Grand Canyon

Text by Nicky Leach
Principal photography by Kerrick James and
Richard Cummins
Series Editor: Tony Halliday

Berlitz POCKET GUIDE

Grand Canyon

First Edition 2006

PHOTOGRAPHY CREDITS
Richard Cummins 11, 21, 24, 29, 49, 59, 62, 63, 64, 67, 68, 70, 71, 72, 96; Tony Halliday 8, 41, 43, 44, 45, 50, 57, 58, 74–5, 76, 87; Kerrick James 6, 10, 17, 18, 22, 27, 30, 32, 35, 37, 38, 47, 48, 53, 55, 60, 66, 77, 78, 80, 81, 84, 88, 89, 91, 92, 94, 97; Anthony Blake Picture Library 103; Cephas/StockFood 101; Laura Rauch/AP/Empics 104; Bob Rowan/Progressive Image/Corbis 83; Smithsonian Institution/Anthropological Archives 14; Smithsonian Institution/National Museum of American Art 13
Cover picture: David Tomlinson/Pictures Colour Library

CONTACTING THE EDITORS
Every effort has been made to provide accurate information in this publication, but changes are inevitable. The publisher cannot be responsible for any resulting loss, inconvenience or injury. We would appreciate it if readers would call our attention to any errors or outdated information by contacting Berlitz Publishing, PO Box 7910, London SE1 1WE, England.
Fax: (44) 20 7403 0290;
e-mail: berlitz@apaguide.co.uk
www.berlitzpublishing.com

 Rafting the Colorado River can be the realization of a dream (page 92)

Stunning scenery awaits hikers descending into the canyon from South Rim (pages 33–5)

A trip to the Hopi Mesas (page 83), home of an ancient and proud culture

TOP TEN ATTRACTIONS

Canyon de Chelly (page 78), visited for its dramatic scenery and Anasazi ruins
▼

Sedona and Oak Creek Canyon (page 72), idyllic country to the south of Flagstaff
◄

The beautiful waterfalls of Havasu Canyon (page 55)
►

Flagstaff (page 59), home to many historic buildings and some good museums
◄

Spectacular Zion Canyon (page 49) lies just over the border in Utah
►

Monument Valley (page 74), the classic Western landscape in the heart of Navajo country
▼

The canyon seen from Bright Angel Point on North Rim (page 44)
▼

CONTENTS

nand Foch, stare at the canyon, then, unable to take it all in, simply say, 'How about a cup of coffee?'

Simply looking, therefore, is not enough to begin to understand. To do that, you'll need to get out of the car, put down your camera or camcorder, and walk around. It helps to arrive at the South Rim – the most developed of the two canyon rims – in the early morning, when it's cooler and parking spaces are easy to find. Or visit any time other than summer, when the tourist season is in full swing. When temperatures soar at the 7,000-ft (2,100-m) South Rim, many find respite at the 8,200-ft (2,460-m) North Rim, the less-visited north side of the canyon. Here you can camp out under vanilla-scented ponderosa pines, walk to overlooks on easy rim trails, and enjoy a grandstand view of the canyon from the stone patio of the lovely Grand Canyon Lodge and its rustic cabins.

After parking, orient yourself to the park by riding one of the shuttle buses that link the Canyon View Information Plaza and Grand Canyon Village with overlooks and trailheads along the West and East Rims. Get on and off to hike

Carving the Canyon

Almost half the earth's 4.5-billion-year history is contained within the colorful horizontal layer cake of sedimentary rocks found within the Grand Canyon, and yet it has taken just a brief moment in geological time (some 4.7 million years) for the action of water, ice and wind to carve out the canyon itself. The Colorado, the 'Red River', was so named by Spaniards for its tawny sediments, and these once tore through the canyon, scouring the river banks. Downcutting has slowed now that the river has reached resistant schists at the bottom of the canyon and its erosive force has been tamed by Glen Canyon Dam, with most of the sediments now ending up at the bottom of Lake Powell.

A traditional dory in the canyon

portions of the easy Rim Trail that stretches for miles along the canyon edge. Stroll along Grand Canyon Village's historic district and take in stunning views as well as exhibits about the human, natural, and geological history of the canyon. If you're fit enough and well prepared, hike a short way below the rim to view the rocks up close. Scan the skies for endangered condors. Get up early to see the sun rise above the canyon. Rent a bike. Ride a mule. Take a one-day scenic railroad trip. Attend a lecture at the Shrine of the Ages Auditorium. Sign up for a class with the Grand Canyon Field Institute. Perhaps even plan a raft trip through the canyon.

At 6,000–8,000ft (1,800–2,400m) in elevation, the area surrounding the Grand Canyon is cold and snow-covered in winter and pleasant in summer, with average temperatures in the 80s Fahrenheit (20s centigrade). Spring arrives in May, with strong winds and changeable weather, while fall is the best time for hiking, when days are still warm and oaks and aspens are changing. It's a different story below the rim. As elevation drops to 3,000ft (900m) – equivalent to a trip to Sonora, Mexico – temperatures climb, allowing cactus, wild flowers and other flora to bloom by April. At summer's height, the inner gorge is soaring to 100°F (37°C) daily, furnace heat that contrasts dramatically with the chilly waters of the Colorado River emerging from the 1963 Glen Canyon Dam upstream.

Beyond North and South Rims

At the junction of Interstates 40 and 17, beneath Arizona's highest mountain, Humphreys Peak, is the historic railroad town of Flagstaff, home of Northern Arizona University. Centrally located in the Northland, it's a good base for day trips in every direction.

To the southeast are the White Mountains, part of the volcanic Mogollon Rim, where Mormons, cowboys and Apache Indians live amid prehistoric ruins and some of the most beautiful forests and lakes in Arizona. Southwest of Flagstaff is artsy Sedona, a paradise for new agers amid scenic red rocks and the shady Oak Creek. Beyond Sedona, above the Verde Valley, is the quaint restored mining town of Jerome, and Prescott, the former state capital, today an old-time cowboy haunt adjoining Prescott Valley, one of Arizona's fastest-growing towns.

Old workings in Jerome

West of Flagstaff, as the Colorado Plateau descends into the Mohave Desert, the Route 66 towns of Williams, Seligman and Kingman have old-fashioned main streets containing old-fashioned roadside neon, down-home diners, and tricked-out roadsters. Just north of Kingman is Grand Canyon West. From Peach Springs, on the Hualapai Reservation, you can take scenic air, motor, and raft tours of the western canyon. Supai, home to the neighboring Havasupai tribe, is inside the canyon itself. It can only be reached by descending on foot or by mule or hiking from the river.

The landscape east of Flagstaff rolls out in high desert grasslands and the shifting hues of the Painted Desert in Petrified Forest National Park. North of Interstate 40, lonesome highways lead to the Hopi Mesas, where Hopi people still live in ancient villages, making handicrafts, performing dances, and dry farming as their ancestors, the Ancestral Pueblo, once did.

The small Hopi reservation is surrounded by the 29,000 sq-mile (72,500 sq-km) Navajo reservation, which spans northeastern Arizona and northwestern New Mexico. There are several spectacular national and tribal parks here, including iconic Monument Valley and Canyon de Chelly National Monument, fascinating not only for its beauty but for its ancient Pueblo ruins and modern Navajo hogans. Almost every family makes turquoise and silver jewelry, rugs, baskets, sand paintings, and folk art, so plan on stopping to shop and getting to know the people whose home this has been for centuries.

Grand Circle Parks

The Grand Canyon is part of a larger geophysical region called the Colorado Plateau, a sprawling, 130,000 sq-mile (325,000 sq-km) highland encompassing parts of Arizona, New Mexico, Colorado and Utah, or Four Corners. The plateau was elevated at the same time as the Rocky Mountains, 65 million years ago. It is now a mile (1.6km) high and still rising, covered in forested volcanic peaks, lava mesas, and eroded buttes, and riddled with labyrinthian sandstone canyons carved by the Colorado and its tributaries. The Grand Canyon is only one of several scenic national parks in Arizona and Utah carved by the Colorado River system. Beyond the North Rim are Zion and Bryce Canyons. Both have distinctive colored rocks eroded dramatically from an ascending 'geological Grand Staircase'.

A BRIEF HISTORY

In 1857, shortly after Mexico ceded most of the Southwest to the United States, government surveyor Lt Joseph 'Christmas' Ives visited the Grand Canyon. 'The region… is of course altogether valueless,' he wrote dismissively in his 1858 report. 'It can be approached only from the south, and after entering it there is nothing to do but leave. Ours has been the first, and will doubtless be the last, party of whites to visit this profitless locality. It seems intended that the Colorado River, along the greater portion of its lonely and majestic way, shall be forever unvisited and undisturbed.'

Perhaps Ives can be forgiven for such a spectacular error in judgment. For centuries, the canyon had been more barrier than attraction to travel. A detachment of Francisco Vásquez

Thomas Moran's *Chasm of the Colorado*, 1873–4

John Wesley Powell with a Paiute scout

de Coronado's Spanish conquistadors, led by Garcia Lopez de Cardenas, had been unable to find a way across on their 1540 expedition and soon left. Spanish fathers Dominguez and Escalante, returning to New Mexico after failing to find a route to Monterey from Santa Fe in 1776, had also avoided the canyon, crossing the Colorado at a ford to the northeast under what is now Lake Powell.

The cross-country trails that brought thousands of travelers west, starting with the Santa Fe Trail in 1821, went to the north via Utah. Stagecoaches and a branch of the transcontinental railroad, which would carry visitors to the Grand Canyon from nearby Williams, were still decades away, and modern roads unimaginable. Only mountain men, prospectors, and local Indians had spent much time in the great chasm. Grand Canyon tourism must have seemed as inconceivable as traveling to the moon.

Opening the West

It would be another 11 years before another Army man, Civil War veteran John Wesley Powell, would make his historic river runs through the canyon. Unlike Ives, Powell's thorough explorations and widely read 1875 report opened the floodgates. Scientists, artists, prospectors, homesteaders, and early concessionaires began to blaze trails through the west, and in short order Yellowstone, Yosemite, and other spectacular landscapes were set aside as national parks.

By the time President Theodore Roosevelt made his trip to the North Rim, in 1903, at the invitation of Mormon businessmen from the North Rim region, the only protection the Grand Canyon and its surrounding national forests had received was as a hunting preserve. His hosts believed the canyon was worthy of national park status, and had already built roads and a cable across the Colorado River at Phantom Ranch to prove their point. After bucketing across on the cable, Roosevelt agreed. In 1908, he used newly created executive powers to declare part of the Grand Canyon a national

John Wesley Powell

In 1869, one-armed Civil War veteran Major John Wesley Powell headed a party of nine men on a daring 900-mile (1,450-km), four-month expedition down the Colorado River, the first to successfully raft the river, from Green River, Wyoming, to the mouth of the Virgin River, west of the Grand Canyon. Rowing four wooden dories, the party negotiated dangerous rapids, portaged long distances around obstacles, survived rockfalls and injuries, suffered severe exposure to the elements, and endured dwindling food supplies. Only six men ultimately completed the journey; the remaining three walked out of the canyon and were mysteriously killed in the Arizona Strip.

Powell's names for canyons, rivers, and geological landmarks remain, such as Glen Canyon, Separation Canyon, and Bright Angel Creek – the latter named for its contrast with the muddy Dirty Devil River. Powell returned to the Grand Canyon two years later to formally survey the region for the government. Headquartered in Kanab, Utah, he befriended Mormons and local Indians, connections that stood the former geology professor in good stead in Washington DC, where he later ran the newly founded US Geological Survey and US Bureau of Ethnology. For more information, visit the John Wesley Powell Museum in Page, adjoining the reservoir that bears Powell's name.

monument. Then in 1919, the park was upgraded to a national park. In 1975, its size was almost doubled. After that, Grand Canyon tourism grew every year, from an initial 45,000 visitors to a hundred times that amount today.

First Peoples

The first native people in the southwest may have come as early as 40,000 years ago. Big game hunters, chasing mammoths through the savannah grasslands and lakes in the late Ice Age probably arrived via the Bering Strait, a land bridge linking Asia and Alaska. Evidence of these Clovis, and later Folsom, hunters appeared south of the Grand Canyon region beginning 13,000 years ago. But only a few spear points belonging to the mobile hunter-gatherers have been found.

Climatic warming and overhunting doomed the mammoths, camels, short-faced bear, giant sloths, and dire wolves. As they disappeared, so too did the big game hunters. In their stead came a more flexible transitional culture, the Archaic, which adapted to changing times in ways that made it one of the southwest's most successful cultures. This people's success lay in its adaptability to a changing landscape. Hunters refined their spear points for killing deer, bighorn sheep, rabbits, and other animals that replaced big game. They invented a spear thrower, or *atlatl,* to improve accuracy. Archaic people became skilled botanists, learning about the hundreds of wild plants that were now appearing on the Colorado Plateau and harvesting them in a seasonal round that took them from mountain to valley. Women processed seeds, pinyon nuts, and other foods with hand stones *(manos)* and grinding blocks *(metates).*

Prehistoric Farmers

About 4,000 years ago, as drought took hold, strange painted images of elongated anthropomorphs, bighorn sheep, and shield-like figures began to appear in deep canyons. Archaeol-

Ancient petroglyphs on Newspaper Rock, Petrified Forest

ogists theorize that they are the work of medicine men journeying to sacred sites to ask for help from the gods. The Shaman's Gallery, below the North Rim of the Grand Canyon, is one of the most famous of these sites. Palm-sized figurines of bighorn sheep and deer made from willow twigs have also been found secreted in caves in the canyon walls. They may have been hunting fetishes. Several are exhibited at Tusayan Museum.

In Mexico, people domesticated a wild grass called *teosinte*, an early precursor to corn, and began to grow seasonal crops in the highlands. Agriculture filtered north about 3,500 years ago, creating a permanent cultural revolution in the southwest. Growing their own food required people to stay in one place and tend harvests. Mobile hunter-gatherers increasingly opted to became sedentary farmers.

The first people to grow corn in the Grand Canyon region were Basketmakers, renowned for their tightly woven baskets. They lived in rock shelters or pithouses roofed with beams

Montezuma's Castle, a spectacular Ancestral Pueblo cliff house

and earth and entered from above via a ladder. Basketmakers lived at Nankoweap Delta inside the Grand Canyon and raised cotton and other crops along the Colorado River 1,300 years ago. They stored crops in slab-lined stone cists and used throwing sticks and bows and arrows for hunting game.

Ancestral Puebloans

Clan joined clan, and eventually hamlets grew into villages. Villagers shared technologies. One of the most important was above-ground architecture. At first, walls were built with *jacal*, a version of wattle and daub using sticks and mortar. These evolved into multi-story room blocks made of mud-mortared stones and roofed with large timber *(viga)* beams latticed with narrow *latillas*. Pithouses were incorporated as underground ceremonial rooms, or *kivas*, with firepits and a hole in the ground *(sipapu)*, that represented the People's Place of Emergence from lower worlds.

The introduction of ceramics from Mexico meant that the native Indian people could make pots in which to store and carry seeds and household items. As they do today, the women in different villages used local clays, and decorated their pots with unique patterns which allowed modern archaeologists to identify them.

In the 1500s, Spanish explorers named these people *Pueblo*, or 'town dwellers'. But different villagers followed different traditions. The Chacoans, whose culture centered on the remote Chaco Canyon in New Mexico, built a powerful civilization that traded throughout the southwest for 200 years. Chaco's power probably derived from its central location as a redistribution center. Another major center was Mesa Verde, a well-watered plateau in southwest Colorado. Mesa Verde-style architecture included lookout towers, probably for defense but also as an aid to tracking the solstices. It is not clear what led residents to build cliff dwellings inside canyon walls in around 1200, whether it was for defense, for better protection from the elements or for a combination of factors.

Pueblos (the word can be applied to the place as well as to the people) in the Grand Canyon region, were influenced by Mesa Verde and Chaco. The Betatakin Pueblo, preserved at Navajo National Monument, represents the most beautiful local expression of the Kayenta culture, which produced less refined architecture than earlier Pueblo cultures. Wupatki Pueblo, near Flagstaff, is an unusual synthesis of Kayenta, Chaco, and local Sinagua masonry styles, as well as exotic

> Cowboy archaeologist Richard Wetherill called the culture he found at Mesa Verde *Anasazi* – a Navajo word for 'enemy ancestors'. The Hopi dislike the use of the word *Anasazi* and use the word *Hisatsinom* to refer to their ancestors. In national parks, you'll find the term Ancestral Pueblo in use today.

southern Hohokam elements such as a large ball court. It was probably a trading pueblo on a cultural frontier. Tusayan Pueblo, a small 13th-century pueblo at the South Rim of the Grand Canyon, is a typical small western Pueblo farming community. Surrounded by neighboring pueblos of similar size, the people of Tusayan grew corn, then later beans and squash, on terraces using dams, irrigation ditches and other devices to retain moisture. Grand Canyon sites have fewer *kivas* than at Chaco or Mesa Verde. The Grand Canyon, it seems, was their great kiva – the original *sipapu*, or place of emergence.

Clear views of the San Francisco Peaks to the south were also important. To the Hopi the peaks are the sacred winter home of the *katsinas,* or spirits, who help to make rain and other blessings. The Navajo, whose reservation surrounds the Hopi Mesas, revere the peaks as one of the four sacred mountains that make up the corners of their world. Landmarks such as these remain important to all of the region's Indian tribes.

By AD1300, a long drought had emptied out the pueblos. Their inhabitants moved to the Hopi Mesas and the Rio Grande settlements in New Mexico. At the same time, Athabascan newcomers from northwest Canada, which split into the Apache and Navajo tribes in the southwest, were filtering into the area. The Apache remained hunter-gatherers in the mountains while the Navajo settled among the Pueblos and learned farming, pottery, and other ways of life.

In the western Grand Canyon, new arrivals from the Mojave Desert included the Cerbat/Pai people, ancestors of today's Hualapai and Havasupai tribes. On the North Rim, Paiute people from the Great Basin of Nevada and Utah mingled with Virgin River people of the Arizona Strip. Undoubtedly the newcomers put pressure on existing tribes but it is still unclear whether it was the deciding factor in causing the abandonment of the pueblos. Today, 14 tribes can trace their ancestry to the Grand Canyon.

Grand Hotel, modeled on a park lodge, schedules a popular nightly dinner show featuring Navajo Indian dancers, and has the only indoor swimming pool at the Grand Canyon.

You can fly into Tusayan from Scottsdale on Grand Canyon Airlines. Scenic air tours over the Grand Canyon leave from the airport daily. They're popular with visitors on a schedule but, environmentally, they have their detractors. The constant noise of overflights disrupts the natural quiet at the canyon and, on some trails, can make you feel as if you're in the city.

The spectacular large-format IMAX film celebrating the Grand Canyon offers a close-up look at the canyon for those unable to descend into it. It is shown hourly on the half hour at the **National Geographic Grand Canyon IMAX Theater and Visitor Center**. A National Geographic photo gallery offers its own inspiring imagery. The Arizona Office of

The Grand Canyon Railway runs daily from Williams

Tourism has a booth inside the theater's entrance and will help you with planning, brochures, and reservations. You can also pay your park entrance fee here.

Orientation

The south entrance to **Grand Canyon National Park** (<www.nps.gov/grca>, open daily, admission fee) is a mile ahead. Although there are several pay booths, lines get long as the day wears on, so try to get there before 10am. The current fee of $20 (£10) per carload includes a five-day pass for South and North Rims; a map/brochure on the natural and cultural history of the park and its attractions; and *The Guide*, a seasonal newspaper with current visitor information, maps, suggestions, and feature articles on the canyon published by the park's non-profit partner, Grand Canyon Association.

Parking at the South Rim has long been an issue, with too few spaces available for large numbers of cars and buses. The park's new transportation plan is designed to ease congestion and prise people from their cars onto routed shuttle buses, the historic train, bicycles, and footpaths. A planned light rail linking Tusayan and the new visitor orientation center at Canyon View Information Plaza, next to Mather Point, is currently on hold. But Grand Canyon Foundation, a non-profit organization charged with raising funds to build a new trail system, has already constructed one greenway and is presently beginning another that will link Tusayan and Grand Canyon Village.

Visitors may park for one hour in the Mather Point parking lot for a first view of the canyon, allowing you enough time to nip across the road to the outdoor **Canyon View Information Plaza** (open 8am–5pm; plaza exhibits open 24 hours), which lies 300yds (275m) through the pinyon-juniper forest on a paved trail. The outdoor information panels on wildlife, geology, hiking and other activies, and indoor ranger desk at the spacious plaza constitute the main park visitor center at

The lobby of the Bright Angel Lodge

present. Heritage Center, slated for the historic buildings surrounding the railroad depot in the village, is not yet built. It will include a new visitor center, museum, and other facilities. The Plaza also has a large bookstore, **Books and More** (open daily 8am–6pm), where you can buy books, maps, and gifts. It is one of several Grand Canyon Association retail outlets at the park with a large, well-chosen selection of items, from guidebooks to plush toys and nature games.

Getting Around

Because parking is so tight at Mather Point, visitors are urged to drive directly to Grand Canyon Village, park in one of the five parking lots there, and return to Canyon View Information Plaza on a free shuttle. The Blue line loops around the village, stopping at **Yavapai Point Observation Station** (open daily 8am–6pm, later in summer), a small museum and bookstore with great views of the canyon through its glass

Descending into the canyon along the South Kaibab Trail

wall. The Green line, from Canyon View Information Plaza, takes you to the **South Kaibab Trail**, one of the two main developed trails into the canyon (the other is Bright Angel Trail). The Red line shuttle leaves from the Village Transfer Station and travels the 8-mile (12-km) West Rim Drive, closed to traffic. Park shuttles run every 15–30 minutes in high season and operate from an hour before sunrise to an hour after sunset.

Consider combining a shuttle ride with some walking, hopping aboard a bus whenever you get tired. The partially paved **Rim Trail** links Hermit's Rest, at the end of West Rim Drive, with Pipe Creek Vista, at the eastern end. Alternatively, the 2-mile (3-km) **Greenway Trail** from the village to Canyon View Information Plaza offers walkers and bicyclists a quiet and pleasant trip through the pine forest.

Grand Canyon Village

The historic center of the South Rim since the late 1800s, Grand Canyon Village is where you'll find all the hotels, restaurants, museums, stores, and other facilities, as well as the **Bright Angel Trail**, leading directly into the canyon.

If you arrive by the historic train from Williams, you'll get out right in the compact center of the village – the way its developers, the Santa Fe Railroad, originally intended. From here, it's an easy stroll to the **El Tovar Hotel**, which was designed in 1905 by Chicago architect Charles Whittlesey. Mary Colter, one of the first women architects in America, did the interior design, using the hotel to experiment with what would become her signature Indian-themed color scheme, motifs, and furnishings. Even if you're not staying there, stroll through the lobby to soak up the atmosphere of backwoods luxury exuding from the comfortable old building, or reserve ahead to enjoy a special meal in the dining room.

The paved rim trail runs in front of El Tovar and **Hopi House**, the Pueblo-style arts and crafts store that was Mary Colter's homage to the Hopi people (many lived and demonstrated their crafts here). As you walk past the architecturally undistinguished modern Thunderbird and Kachina Lodges, look down to the ledges immediately below the rim. This is a favored haunt of reintroduced endangered condors, which fly hundreds of miles from their Arizona Strip release site on the North Rim in search of carrion. On particularly windy days, when flying on the thermals is too difficult, you'll count up numerous birds resting there. Free ranger talks about the condor program are offered at this location most afternoons. Other ranger programs take place at El Tovar, Canyon View Information Plaza, Yavapai Observation Station, Lipan Point, Tusayan Museum, Desert View, and Phantom Ranch and the Shrine of Ages.

The condors are easy to see below **Lookout Studio**, on the rim's edge, and nearby **Bright Angel Lodge**, both designed by Mary Colter. The lodge's bar, soda fountain, and restaurant are popular lunchtime haunts with

Grand Canyon architect Mary Jane Elizabeth Colter was so particular about the shade of blue used for the interior trim at Bright Angel Lodge, painters dubbed it 'Mary Jane Blue'.

The Hopi House

famished hikers stretching out sore muscles on the patio after returning from an early morning hike down the nearby Bright Angel Trail. Enter the cool, dark building and you'll see a dramatic thunderbird, which Colter called 'the bright angel of the sky', hung above the mantelpiece of the lobby's huge fireplace.

There is another interesting fireplace in the old lounge, now a museum containing delightful memorabilia from the heyday of Fred Harvey and his famous Harvey Girls. Dominating the room, a 10-ft (3-m) high 'geological fireplace' contains all of the 1.8 billion years of rock formations in the Grand Canyon in sequence, from top to bottom: fossil-rich creamy Kaibab Limestone, calcareous Toroweap Formation, white dune-formed Coconino Sandstone, red mud Hermit Shale, the ledgy Supai Group, marine-formed Redwall Limestone, purplish Temple Butte Limestone, oceanic Muav Limestone, silty Bright Angel Shale, dark brown Tapeats Sandstone, and dark volcanic Vishnu Schist shot through with pink-striped Zoreaster Granite.

Into the Canyon

Bright Angel Trail, developed as a trail by miners Pete Berry and Ralph Cameron, has been the most popular trail into the canyon since 1891, when Cameron opened a toll booth charging tourists to enter the canyon. It begins just below **Kolb Studio** (open 8am–6pm), the former photography studio belonging to the Kolb brothers, which in 1904 was restored and converted into a bookstore and art gallery.

Beginning in 1904, the Kolbs made their living photographing tourists descending into the canyon. In the early morning, they'd snap the customers astride their mules, then either Ellsworth or Emory Kolb would run 3,000ft (900m) down Bright Angel Trail to Indian Gardens, 4½ miles (7km) below, to get water to develop the pictures for pickup later that day. Today, dude wranglers still lead mule strings down to Indian Creek, onto the broad Tonto Platform, then descend into the Inner Canyon to **Phantom Ranch**, a 1922 rustic hideaway designed by Mary Colter and located on Bright Angel Creek.

Hiking the Canyon

Water piped from the North Rim to the South Rim via a pipeline is available on Bright Angel Trail. This water is particularly important to hikers during the canyon's bone-dry summers, when temperatures below the rim soar to 100°F (37°C) and the effort of climbing out of the canyon can quickly lead to heat exhaustion or stroke without adequate hydration. All the canyon's trails are rocky, dry, steep, and challenging, and not to be undertaken without preparation. Even if you're going a short way, carry and drink a gallon of water per person along with salty high-energy foods, and wear sturdy hiking boots, a broad-brimmed hat, a wet bandanna around the neck, and cover exposed skin. Don't rush it. Hike slowly, rest in the heat of day, and allow three times as long to climb out as to hike in. Your survival may depend on it.

To reach the river, plan on an overnight hike to the bottom of the canyon, where you can rent a bunk at Phantom Ranch or sleep in a designated backcountry campsite. Under no circumstances try to hike the 24 miles (38km) to the river and back in one day. Distances are deceptive, and it is usually fit hikers pushing their bodies too hard who get into trouble and end up needing to be rescued. For information on trail conditions, check at Canyon View Information Plaza, the **Backcountry Office** (tel: 928-638-7875), or call the **Park Information Line** (tel: 928-638-7888).

West Rim Drive

Other South Rim trails, mostly undeveloped former miners' trails, should not be undertaken without experience in desert hiking. But 6½-mile (10.5-km) **Hermit Trail**, at the end of the West Rim Drive, is an exception. It offers a pleasant day's hike into a beautiful side canyon that leads to French-Canadian prospector Louis Boucher's old camp at Dripping Springs. The rocky path descends from the Kaibab Limestone to the red-and-gray Toroweap Formation, through pinyon, juniper, and netleaf hackberry. On quiet days, listen for tuneful canyon wrens singing among the rocks.

You can buy cold drinks and sit on the porch and relax at **Hermit's Rest**, another of Mary Colter's delightful buildings. The West Rim shuttle stops at eight overlooks, allowing you to get on and off and walk portions of the Rim Trail which, beyond **Maricopa Point** becomes rocky and undeveloped. The massive formation known as the **Battleship** is best seen from this overlook. Geologist Clarence Dutton gave many of the buttes, or 'temples' as he called them, exotic names like Isis, Shiva, Brahma, and Osiris. From **Mohave Point**, on a still day, you can hear the muffled roar of crashing waves at Granite and Hermit Rapids on the Colorado and imagine John Wesley Powell's epic journey in 1869.

Desert View Drive

One of the park's best-kept secrets is 25-mile (40-km) long **Desert View Drive** along the East Rim (Highway 64). The drive heads east from Pipe Creek Vista, and overlooks along the way some spectacular scenery. From **Yaki Point** the panorama includes the massive beveled surface of **Wotans Throne**, and beside it graceful, pointed **Vishnu Temple**. The 7-mile **South Kaibab Trail** departs from near Yaki Point, snaking down the side of **O'Neill Butte** through a break in the Redwall Limestone, down to Bright Angel Campground and Phantom Ranch. It's also a good choice for a short day hike to **Cedar Point**, but has no shade and is very steep.

Other overlooks offer glimpses of a canyon that begins to look quite different as you follow the path of the Colorado River out of the deepest part of the Grand Canyon into the

Riding mules from Phantom Ranch along the South Kaibab Trail

Captain John Hance, Grand Canyon's first white settler, arrived at Grand Canyon in 1883 and lived there until his death in 1919. He built a guest ranch east of Grandview Point and several trails, many of which followed old Havasupai trails.

Painted Desert and Navajo Reservation beyond.

Grandview Point looks down on the Horseshoe Mesa, site of early copper mines. The **Grandview Trail** starts here, built by miners to reach the ore. But even a short walk reveals that hauling it out could never be a profitable enterprise, even for top quality ore. Grandview was among the first destinations for early tourists to the canyon, who stayed at Pete Berry's Grandview Hotel.

Be sure to stop at **Tusayan Museum** (open daily 9am–5pm, admission free) located beside an excavated 12th-century village built by ancestors of today's Hopi people, who live on the mesas to the east. A self-guided trail takes you a mile (1.6km) around the pueblo to view room blocks, kivas, crop terraces, and wild plants like yucca, juniper, and pinyon that were used by prehistoric people.

Lipan Point has one of the most expansive views of the canyon and Colorado River. In the fall, hundreds of hawks – Cooper's, sharpshins, redtails, and others – migrate over this overlook on their way south. Nearby, in 1540, Spanish conquistadors tried unsuccessfully to enter the canyon.

The last stop in the park – and perhaps the most extraordinary – is **Desert View** itself, which has a bookstore/park information center (open daily 9am–5pm), a gift shop, restrooms, and a large parking lot. Climb to the top of Mary Colter's unusual **Watchtower,** built in 1932, for extraordinary views of the Painted Desert to the east, the wide Marble Platform, and the Navajo reservation. You'll be equally amazed by the painted murals by Hopi artist Fred Kabotie, which line the walls. Nowhere in the park feels quite as authentically 'Indian' as the Watchtower, inspired by Mesa Verde-style Pueblo architecture found throughout the region.

The Little Colorado

The Navajo reservation begins just a few miles farther east. **Little Colorado River Navajo Tribal Park** sits at an overlook above the dark gorge of the Little Colorado River, near where it joins the main river.

It is at the Little Colorado River that we encounter one of the greatest conundrums concerning the creation of

The Little Colorado

the Grand Canyon. The massive upwarp of the Kaibab Plateau began to lift around 35 million years ago, effectively creating a barrier to the Colorado River on its journey west. Why, then, does the river appear to have cut through this high ground rather than go round it? Geologists theorize that the Little Colorado may now occupy the original route of the Colorado as it wound its way southeast of the Kaibab Plateau. Another stream flowed west of the plateau and cut back into it, in a process known as headwater erosion, eventually 'capturing' the Colorado, which turned westward to its present position through the newer, steeper route. At this point, the sediment-heavy waters began to carve the chasm, probably within the last 4.7 to 1.7 million years *(see also page 9)*.

Running through Marble Canyon

SOUTH RIM TO NORTH RIM

The five-hour drive from the South Rim of the Grand Canyon to its North Rim, via Highway 89 and 89A, offers the chance to appreciate this beautiful high desert landscape. Just beyond the junction of Highways 64 and 89 is **Cameron,** at the Little Colorado River crossing, where a bustling trading post has served the Navajo reservation for a century. Gas, food, and lodging are available. Inside the post you can buy Indian crafts or sample Navajo tacos and other fare in the tin-ceilinged dining room.

Marble Canyon

After a brief drive through the Western Navajo reservation, you leave it at **Marble Canyon,** where, in 1929, the 467-ft (140-m) high Navajo Bridge made history as the highest steel structure in the world and the only bridge over the Colorado River for 600 miles (965km). A wider bridge opened in 1997.

Park at **Navajo Bridge Visitor Center**, part of **Glen Canyon National Recreation Area** *(see page 48)* and walk over the old bridge for great views. A handsome interpretive center, echoing Pueblo architecture, sells books and offers information on nearby Lake Powell and Glen Canyon Dam. Behind the 2,000-ft (600-m) high Vermilion Cliffs is **Lees Ferry**, once a ferry crossing operated by the famous Mormon elder, John D. Lee. Today, it's the put-in for Grand Canyon river trips, and the take-out for floats from the dam to Lees Ferry. Lee's old homestead, **Lonely Dell**, is a historic site.

Vermilion Cliffs

Highway 89A continues to the base of the Kaibab Plateau, on a route pioneered by Spanish fathers Dominguez and Escalante in 1776. It passes **House Rock Valley**, a grassy break in the cliffs long used by Kaibab Paiutes and later, Mormon ranchers. Today it runs past the 293,000-acre (119,000-hectare) **Vermilion Cliffs National Monument**, incorporating the **Paria Canyon-Vermilion Cliffs Wilderness**. The wilderness has three spectacular slot canyons – narrow sandstone passageways carved by streams. The most popular is the 38-mile (61-km) **Paria River Canyon** to **Paria, Utah**, a trip of four to six days. The southern trailhead

As you drive past House Rock Valley, look out for a herd of buffalo that lives here. The original herd was driven to Arizona by Jesse 'Buffalo' Jones, an aging buffalo hunter. In the early 1900s, Jones hoped (fruitlessly) to save the last remaining buffalo by cross-breeding them with cattle. Jones served as hunting guide for western writer Zane Grey in 1907 and was later immortalized in Grey's classic *Last of the Plainsmen*.

is at Lees Ferry. Day users must register before setting out; all overnight trips are by permit only, with daily quotas in force. The best time to do this river hike (which requires wading in places) is mid-March to June. This is not the place to be during a flash flood in a summer monsoon. For more information, contact the Bureau of Land Management (BLM) in Kanab, Utah (open Mon–Fri 7.45am–4.30pm, tel: 435-644-4600).

The Historic Arizona Strip

Highway 89A winds onto the 8,000-ft (2,400-m) high **Kaibab Plateau**, through old-growth ponderosa pine forest clinging to Kaibab Limestone. The main services for the plateau are at **Jacob Lake**, named for Mormon missionary Jacob Hamblin, who came through here on a proselytizing mission to the Hopi Indians in the 1860s.

Mormon history is rich in the quiet ranch country of the Arizona Strip, a narrow swathe of land between the North Rim of the Grand Canyon and the Vermilion Cliffs which, until John Wesley Powell conducted a survey here in 1871, was thought to be part of adjoining Utah. For centuries before whites arrived, Ancestral Pueblo people and later Paiutes traveled to the North Rim each summer to hunt mule, deer, elk, and other game. Paiutes collected agave inside the canyon and roasted it for ceremonies. In the mid-1860s, Navajos used the canyon to hide from Lt Kit Carson's soldiers during the tragic Long Walk that forced the tribe to leave their homelands and

> In 1892, Buffalo Bill escorted a party of wealthy English nobles interested in game hunting and ranching in the Arizona Strip. They stopped for a meal at Jacob Lake, where Buffalo Bill reputedly said grace at one meal, offering thanks for many blessings, specifically 'Emma Bentley's custard pie'.

walk to a concentration camp in eastern New Mexico. During the Civil War, starving Navajos and a few Paiute accomplices would make raids on early Mormon ranchers homesteading at Pipe Spring and other settlements in the Arizona Strip, stealing cattle and killing families, until Jacob Hamblin and John Wesley Powell negotiated a peace settlement in the early 1870s.

Parked up at Jacob Lake

Franklin Woolley, followed by his brother Edwin 'Dee' Woolley, a Kanab businessman, began exploring the plateau's potential for lumber, grazing, and Mormon settlement in 1866. They built a sawmill and cabins and grazed their cattle here in the summer, but the plateau's remoteness, hard winters, and lack of surface water due to limestone sinkholes impeded development. Among Woolley's schemes for developing the area was one to interest English noblemen in game hunting and ranching (even hiring Buffalo Bill in 1892 to escort them by stagecoach from Flagstaff). When much of the North Kaibab was withdrawn as the new Grand Canyon Forest Reserve, in 1893, Woolley and brothers-in-law Henry Bowman and David Rust improved the steep trail from the North Rim to Bright Angel Creek, now known as the North Kaibab Trail, and constructed a short-lived cable car across the river at present-day Phantom Ranch.

> **Kaibab means
> 'mountain lying down'
> in the Paiute language.**

It was this cable that President Teddy Roosevelt rode when he made his famous trip to the Grand Canyon in 1903. He took the newly completed Santa Fe Railroad to the South Rim and cabled across to the North Rim for a hunting expedition with Jim Owen, then a famed mountain lion hunter. Owen, a former member of the Jesse James Gang, boasted that he had killed 532 mountain lions on the plateau. In 1906, Roosevelt appointed him game warden of the new 612,736-acre (248,000 hectares) Grand Canyon Game Reserve, withdrawn from the forest reserve. Thus began a long process that led to the plateau being separated into national forest and national park in 1919.

Jacob Lake to the North Rim

Jacob Lake Inn, at the junction of Highways 89A and 67, is still operated by descendants of Woolley and Bowman. The log inn is a cozy, family-oriented place, still famous for its home-made pies and milk shakes and is the only lodging open year round (and usually mobbed in the fall hunting season). Light sleepers may prefer the 1926 **Kaibab Lodge**, 5 miles 8km) from the park entrance and open only in summer.

At Jacob Lake, the small log US Forest Service **Kaibab Plateau Visitor Center** has exhibits and information on visiting the rough backcountry of the North Kaibab. Dispersed primitive camping (requiring total self-sufficiency) is allowed throughout the little-used Kaibab National Forest, affording lots of solitude and hiking. Ask about the trail to **Snake Gulch**, a remarkable rock art site at the bottom of a canyon, used by Ancestral Pueblo and Paiute Indians. Developed camping and horseback riding are available close to the inn.

Scenic Highway 67, closed by snow between November and May, winds 44 miles (70km) from Jacob Lake to the

North Rim, through dense forests of ponderosa, aspen, and fir interspersed with meadows dotted with Indian paintbrush, lupine, penstemon, shooting star and other wildflowers from June onwards. Look for the tassel-eared Kaibab squirrel, the white-tailed cousin of the Coconino Plateau's darker Abert squirrel, whose destinies diverged when the river carved the deep canyon several million years ago.

Orientation at the North Rim

Because of the short season and isolation, the North Rim has never been as fully developed as the South Rim. You'll find a lovely airy campground beneath the ponderosa pines, a visitor center, a post office, a gas station with a mechanic, a cafeteria, rustic cabins, and the 1937 **Grand Canyon Lodge**, a magnificent stone-and-timber structure designed by Gilbert Stanley Underwood in the Rustic Archi-

Grand Canyon Lodge

Along the Cape Royal Road

tecture style. The picture window makes the lodge dining room a memorable place for what would otherwise be a meal of standard park food.

The 3-mile (5-km) round-trip **Transept Trail** along the forest edge next to Transept Canyon links the campground and lodge. It makes a wonderful after-dinner sunset walk, as soaringly lovely as the cathedral reference in its name, filled with the sounds of squirrels and jays squabbling over seeds and the wind sawing through the lofty pines.

For relaxation and some serious canyon watching, there's no better place than the stone veranda of Grand Canyon Lodge, with its rustic rockers and views of clouds throwing shadows on the yawning abyss below. The half-mile trail to **Bright Angel Point** follows a narrow headland to an overlook poised above the dramatic 4,000-ft (1,200-m) dropoff into **Bright Angel Canyon**, a tributary of the main canyon. It's hard to believe that such a vast space is merely a side branch. The north side's greater depth and intricacy are a product of the asymmetrical carving of the Kaibab Plateau by the Colorado River and the higher elevation, which allows more water to flow into the canyon than away from it, carving steeper side canyons.

Stop at the **North Rim Visitor Center** (open mid-May to mid-October 8am–6pm), adjacent to the parking lot on Bright Angel Peninsula, for park and regional information, maps, brochures, and exhibits. Interpretive programs are offered seasonally.

North Rim Drives and Trails

For a different perspective, plan on driving the **Cape Royal Road** east to **Cape Royal**, a 25-mile (40km) drive that will take at least a half day, with stops at 8,803-ft (2,640-m) **Point Imperial** and other stunning viewpoints along the way. At the end, the 1-mile (1.6-km) round-trip **Cape Royal Trail** offers drivers a chance to stretch their legs, with views of the main canyon, Angels Window, the Colorado River, the Painted Desert, and the Navajo reservation. Markers along the trail interpret the area's natural history. If you have a four-wheel drive, consider driving to **Point Sublime**, the westernmost of the North Rim viewpoints. Inquire about road conditions and possible closures before heading out. This is a very rough road. Allow two hours.

North Kaibab Trail, the main trail into the canyon, is by any hiker's standards, a real must-do, with steep

Flora at the rim

dropoffs much of the way. The return trip to the river and back is 28 miles (45km) and definitely cannot be achieved in one day. If you want to hike this trail in summer, start at dawn, find shade during the midday heat, and make a reservation to overnight at Phantom Ranch.

Mules also use the trail. If the long-haul mule trips down Bright Angel Trail on the South Rim intimidate you, consider doing a shorter ride on the North Rim. One-hour rides along the rim and half-day rim or inner-canyon trips are usually available on a daily basis. Full-day trips into the canyon include lunch. Register in the lobby of Grand Canyon Lodge with **Grand Canyon Trail Rides** (advance reservations, tel: 435-679-8665, desk open 7am–5pm daily, <www.canyon rides.com/pkgrandcanyon.html>).

Hiking stages of the North Kaibab Trail will give you a feel for it without going the whole hog. The 1½-mile (2.4-km) round-trip hike to **Coconino Overlook** and the 4-mile (6-km) round-trip to **Supai Tunnel** are possibilities, as is the 5-mile (8-km) round-trip hike on **Uncle Jim Trail**, which meanders through the forest as far as the steep switchbacks into the canyon. The 9-mile (14-km) round-trip scramble to **Roaring Springs**, the water source for both rims, will take all day, drops 3,050ft (915m), and is best left to the experienced canyon hikers. Artist Bruce Aiken, well-known for his luminous contemporary paintings of the canyon, has lived with his family near Roaring Springs for decades.

Approximately four dozen California condors now fly over northern Arizona after a successful captive breeding program. Condors are often confused with a more common carrion eater: the buzzard or vulture. The main difference is that condors have a 9-ft (3-m) wingspans; buzzard wings are smaller with a distinct V-shape.

The pink cliffs of Bryce Canyon

IN AND OUT OF UTAH

From Jacob Lake, the road spirals 3,000ft (900m) off the plateau, descending from ponderosa pine into pygmy forest of juniper and pinyon. Every five to seven years, pinyon trees produce bumper crops of nuts. Since prehistoric times, people have gathered these nuts in the fall.

Views of the western Arizona Strip and southwestern Utah's Color Country are breathtaking from the **Le Fevre Overlook**. From here you can see the Grand Staircase, an eroded geological 'staircase' of colorful, ascending rock formations, including the Vermilion Cliffs, the White Cliffs of Zion National Park, and the Pink Cliffs of Bryce Canyon – two of the Grand Circle of parks that stretch across southern Utah.

Glen Canyon National Recreation Area

Kanab, so popular with western movie directors in the Forties that it was dubbed 'Little Hollywood', is well situated at the junction of Highways 89A and 89 and has several good restaurants, a handful of reasonable lodgings, and one great little coffee shop/bookstore. Turn east on Highway 89 to visit the Grand Staircase section of Grand Staircase-Escalante National Monument and adjoining **Glen Canyon National Recreation Area** (open daily 7am–4pm, admission fee), which includes 180-mile (290-km) long **Lake Powell**, the second largest man-made lake in the western hemisphere. This is a favorite vacation spot for millions of water-starved desert dwellers each year. Miles of blue water and a 1,961-mile (3,156-km) shoreline of carved sandstone cliffs are used by boaters, water skiiers and jet skiers, kayakers, campers and hikers. There are six marinas. Three of them – two on the Arizona side and one on the Utah side – offer full services for boaters, from houseboat and kayak rentals to lodgings, restaurants, convenience stores, and boat repair.

The lake was created by **Glen Canyon Dam**, constructed between 1956 and 1962 at **Page**, the company town that housed workers and now has the main services for the lake. The 710-ft (220-m) high dam, operated by the US Bureau of Reclamation, generates 1,200 megawatts of hydroelectricity for Phoenix residents. Tours of the dam are offered daily from the adjoining **Carl Hayden Visitor Center** (open daily 8am–6pm in summer, to 5pm for the rest of the year, admission fee), which has exhibits, interpretive presentations, and information on hiking the many side canyons that are now being exposed by drought-caused low-water conditions.

Rainbow Bridge

GRAND CANYON WEST

Immediately opposite Grand Canyon-Parashant National Monument, on the South Rim, is **Grand Canyon West**, a growing tourist development on the **Hualapai Reservation**. The western end of the Grand Canyon, east of Hoover Dam (just before the Colorado River turns south along the state border to form what's known as Arizona's West Coast), offers a very different experience from the main Grand Canyon.

Grand Canyon Resort is aimed at tourists arriving from the West who want a quick visit to the Grand Canyon. Las Vegas, in Nevada to the northwest, and Kingman and Peach Springs, both in Arizona off Interstate 40 on old Route 66, are all two and a half hours away. Small commuter airlines offer day trips directly to Grand Canyon West Airport from Flagstaff and Las Vegas.

A pack train arrives in Supai

The Hualapai Reservation

The Hualapai tribe have already built a casino and a large hotel, and campgrounds are also planned for Grand Canyon Resort. At present, **Hualapai Lodge** (tel: 888-255-9550), in the small tribal headquarters community of **Peach Springs**, is the only lodging available. A variety of day tours may be reserved through the concierge desk; 24 hours' notice is required.

Scenic helicopter rides are offered daily from the airport. Hualapai Tours offers a popular van tour into the Grand Canyon with guides who share information about their culture with visitors. The tour stops at dramatic overlooks like **Eagle Point**, 4,300ft (1,290m) above the river, and travels **Diamond Creek Road**, the only route into the Grand Canyon. Smooth-water pontoon boat tours on the Colorado by **The River Runners** (tel: 888-255-9550) allow you to experience all of the above by flying into the canyon by helicopter and boarding an eight-passenger motorized boat on the river (March through October). At **Grand Canyon Caverns** (open daily; admission fee), you can ride an elevator 21 stories below ground for a 45-minute tour of some limestone caverns.

> Eagle Point is the site of the Grand Canyon Skywalk, an observation deck that juts 75ft (23m) out over the canyon. The platform is mostly made of 4-in (10-cm) thick Plexiglass, allowing visitors a clear view of the Colorado River 4,000ft (1,200m) below. Opened in 2006, the sleek structure has been designed to withstand earthquakes and 100mph (160kph) winds.

The Havasupai Reservation

The Hualapai live just west of their distant cousins, the Havasupai who, like them, once hunted and gathered on the plateau but also farmed inside the canyon. In 1882, the government allocated a 518-acre (209-hectare) reservation for the Havasupai inside the Grand Canyon. The loss of their traditional rim-top lands heavily impacted on the tribe. Fortunately, their location inside the canyon allowed them to capitalize on growing tourism, particularly river-running

Havasu Canyon

through the Grand Canyon. In 1975, 185,000 acres (74,800 hectares) of their original hunting grounds were restored to the tribe but tourism remains the mainstay.

Supai, the tribal headquarters, is home to 450 Havasupai. It may only be reached on foot and horseback from the rim, but is a regular stop for river-runners on the Colorado, who stop to swim in **Havasu Canyon**. The idyllic waterfalls and beautiful, warm blue-green waters of this side canyon gave the tribe their name: People of the Blue Green Waters. In Supai, you'll find the charming 24-room **Supai Lodge** (tel: 928-448-2111; no phones or TVs), a cafe, a campground, a store, a tourist office, and tour companies offering horseback tours from the rim to the village, and from the village to the waterfalls. The descent to the village begins at **Hualapai Hilltop**, the trailhead into the canyon. It has no services, including water. The nearest gas, food, and lodging are 68 miles (108km) away.

Hiking to Havasu

If you're planning on hiking to Supai from Hualapai Hilltop, plan carefully. It's 8 miles (12km) to the village on a steep trail, with 1.5 miles (2.4km) of switchbacks shared with mules. From Supai, it's another 2 miles (3km) to the campground, an additional 3 miles (5km) to Beaver Falls, and 5 miles (8km) to the river. Entry to Havasu Canyon is restricted and by fee only. Wear sturdy hiking boots on the trails, appropriate clothing, and bring a gallon of water per person per day.

Route 66 Towns

Peach Springs is on **Route 66**, the 2,448-mile (3,940-km) highway that was built in 1926 to link the Midwest with California. Much of the long-deteriorated road disappeared under Interstate 40, and was closed in 1985. But you can still see preserved segments in northern Arizona. Neon-lit motels and diners, flashy roadsters, road museums, jukeboxes playing 'Get Your Kicks on Route 66' are found in Flagstaff, Seligman, Oatman, and Kingman, where Route 66 remains the main thoroughfare through town.

The Mother Road

For nearly 60 years, Route 66 was a rite of passage for thousands of travelers. During the Depression, carloads of penniless Dust Bowl immigrants from Oklahoma and Arkansas headed west to California to escape grinding poverty. In the late 1940s, the road brought returning GIs back to Sunbelt cities like Albuquerque and Phoenix, where they had been stationed during World War II. In the 1950s, Beat poets and writers like Jack Kerouac criss-crossed the country, seeking inspiration in the heartland. And in the 1960s, vacationing families in station wagons used the road to reach the Grand Canyon and other western national parks.

Kingman

The sprawling city of **Kingman** at the intersection of Highway 93 and Interstate 40, 48 miles (77km) east of the California border, sits right at the edge of the Mohave Desert. A former turquoise mining center and railroad stop, the modern town is bland and undistinguished architecturally, but the old downtown next to the railroad preserves an extensive section of Route 66 and more than 60 buildings are on the National Register of Historic Places.

Silo sign in Kingman

Stop at **Powerhouse Visitor Center** (120 West Andy Devine Boulevard, open Mon–Fri 9am–6pm) to pick up information and tour the **Route 66 Museum**, which has old cars and other memorabilia. Just around the corner is **Mohave Museum of History and Arts** (400 West Beale Street, open Mon–Fri 9am–5pm, Sat 1pm–5pm; admission fee). The museum displays wagons, mining equipment, farm machinery, a wooden 19th-century Santa Fe Railroad caboose, and an exhibit honoring famed cowboy actor Andy Devine, who grew up in Kingman and has a boulevard named for him.

Oatman

About 25 miles (40km) southwest of Kingman, on Route 66, is **Oatman**, a revived mining town with a dusty western flavor and lots of tourist shops. The town's main attractions are the friendly miners' *burros* (mules), which wander through town, posing for a photo for the price of a carrot. Before leaving, visit the informal museum in the dilapidated **Oatman Hotel**. The hotel's claim to fame is that it was where actors Clark Gable and Carole Lombard spent their wedding night after their spur-of-the-moment wedding in Kingman in 1939.

Seligman

If you're headed to the Hualapai and Havasupai Reservations from the east, you'll leave Interstate 40 at **Seligman**, another great little Route 66 town that seems caught in a time warp. It's great fun strolling the main street of this historic town and taking in its neon-lit motels, diners, and gas station signs. Stop at the **Snow Cap Drive-In**, a popular hamburger joint, for some Happy Days-style nostalgia.

Retro colors at Mr. D'z Route 66 Diner in Kingman

FLAGSTAFF AND ENVIRONS

The railroad is the beating heart of **Flagstaff** (pop. 60,000), the commercial center of the Northland. Running parallel to Interstate 40 and historic Route 66, freight trains and the twice-daily Amtrak passenger train *Southwest Chief* speed noisily through the center of the town, causing north-south traffic to grind to a halt numerous times daily.

Flagstaff, established 1882

The train theme is everywhere. Engine No. 12, a 1929 black steam locomotive that operated in the Flagstaff area in the 1950s, sits outside the Arizona Historical Society's Pioneer Museum *(see page 64)*. One of Flag's hippest coffee houses is named Late for the Train. And even the **Flagstaff Visitor Center** (open Mon–Sat 7am–6pm, Sun 5pm) is headquartered in a section of the train station.

Park west of downtown, next to **Thorpe Park**, which has a small recreation center, and enjoy a walk on downtown's excellent **Urban Trail System**. The short, steep walk up adjoining **Mars Hill** offers the best views of historic Flagstaff and trains passing through town, their sharp whistles bouncing off the foothills of the **San Francisco Peaks**, Arizona's tallest mountain range.

Astronomic Flagstaff

The road dead-ends at **Lowell Observatory** (open 9am–5pm daily; noon–5pm in winter; admission free), founded in

The Lowell Observatory (above) needs dark skies, a commodity which the city of Flagstaff fiercely protects. Only 10 percent of the world's population are now able to see the stars, due to environmental pollution and artificial street lighting.

1894 by wealthy Boston astronomer Percival Lowell who, in 1930, discovered the planet Pluto here. Lowell Observatory's **Steele Visitor Center** and **Slipher Building** have fascinating interactive exhibits on the work of astronomers and the history of the observatory. A short interpretive trail leads to the building holding Lowell's original Clark telescope. During Flagstaff's popular 10-day **Festival of Science** in the fall, and at other times of year, the telescope is available to visitors for periodic star gazing.

More recently, the observatory hit the headlines when the late astronomer and geologist Eugene Shoemaker and his wife Caroline were the first to identify the Shoemaker-Levy Comet. The Shoemakers made their home in Flagstaff, attracted by the fellowship of other scientists in the area, including those at the **US Geological Survey**, which has a campus at the entrance to **Buffalo Park**, a large grassy park off Cedar Avenue with lovely peak views and trails.

Geologists study the surrounding San Francisco Volcanic Field, the largest volcanic field in the continental United States. Gene Shoemaker's geologic specialty was meteors. Just east of Flagstaff, an iron meteor 100ft (30m) in diameter and weighing 60,000 tons hit the earth at 45,000 miles (72,000km) an hour about 50,000 years ago, leaving a 4,000-ft (1,200-m) wide **Meteor Crater** (open daily 6am–6pm in summer, 8am–5pm in winter; admission fee). A visitor center above the crater offers great views.

Historic Flagstaff

Sheepman Thomas McMillan arrived in fall 1876, and became Flagstaff's first official permanent settler. When the Santa Fe Railroad puffed into town in 1882, fresh meat as well as wool could then be sold to markets back east, giving Flagstaff the boost it needed to grow into a lively boardwalk town next to the train tracks and permanent springs. The small **Plaza Vieja** city park at the western end of Coconino Avenue is now the only reminder of the early town.

Businessmen joined sheep herders, railroad workers, and cattle ranchers making (and losing) small fortunes financing business ventures and opening banks, saloons, hotels, stores, restaurants and other services. One pioneer, merchant P.J. Brannen, built a store farther east, next to the railroad depot in what was called New Town; the train station is still in use today.

How Flagstaff got its Name

Long before Percival Lowell arrived in Flagstaff, another group of Bostonians made their mark on Flagstaff, when they passed through northern Arizona in search of good farmland. The would-be colonists arrived at the base of the Peaks in time to celebrate the nation's centennial, on 4 July 1776, by running a flag up a ponderosa pine tree. The flagstaff gave the town its name, when it was officially founded in 1882, the year the railroad reached the community. The flagpole can still be seen near Thorpe Park.

The five Babbitt brothers from Cincinnati, Ohio, were among the most successful entrepreneurs, running so many stock on the grasslands surrounding Flagstaff that locals joked even the sheep said 'Baa-bitt'. Descendants of the original brothers remain a political force today, including former Arizona Governor Bruce Babbitt.

The abundance of old-growth ponderosa pine trees made fortunes for lumbermen Timothy and Michael Riordan, whose stunning 1904 log-and-stone home is preserved as **Riordan State Historic Park** (open daily 8am–5pm summer, 11am–5pm winter; hourly tours; admission fee) in the old millworkers' community of Mill Town – now Milton Road, the town's main southern commercial artery. Designed by Charles Whittlesey (architect for El Tovar Hotel at the Grand Canyon South Rim), the mansion is split into two sets of living quarters for the brothers and their families and is filled with antiques.

Wares from an Indian craft store

Many of Flagstaff's historic buildings and sites have been preserved by an active Main Street Historic Program, which works to keep the historic character of the old downtown. Tiny **Heritage Square**, surrounded by old and new brick buildings at the corner of San Francisco and Aspen Streets, is a new addition. The small amphitheater has

Heritage Square

free concerts nearly every weekend throughout the summer and fall. Opposite Heritage Square is the 1900 **Weatherford Hotel**, one of Flagstaff's most important historic buildings. Like other downtown structures, the two-story hotel was built from locally quarried sandstone called Arizona Red. The newly reopened second-story balcony is a great place to have a drink and to people-watch on a warm summer's evening. Writer Zane Grey rented a turret room in the hotel and wrote *Call of the Canyon* here.

Veteran local historians and prolific authors Richard and Sherry Mangum offer daily historic tours of downtown. Ask at the visitor center for information.

Northern Arizona University

Flagstaff today attracts an interesting mix of small business owners, cowboys, local Indians, writers, photographers, artists, travelers, river-runners, young Rastas, mountain men, and students. By far the greatest number are here to study. About 15,000 students attend **Northern Arizona University**, whose campus is just south of downtown next to Riordan Mansion. Founded in 1899 as a Normal School for teachers, the university still turns out many of the state's teachers and is also known for its anthropology, forestry, and environmental science schools. Cultural events abound here, many of which are held at **Ardrey Auditorium**, home to the Flagstaff Symphony. The university also hosts a busy series of public lectures by visiting authors, scientists, and others.

Museums off Highway 180

Take Humphreys Avenue north from Route 66 and turn left onto Fort Valley Road (Highway 180), where there are several worthwhile museums off the road leading to the Grand Canyon. In addition to a steam locomotive, the aforementioned **Pioneer Museum** (open Mon–Sat 9am–5pm; admission fee) – the former county hospital – displays Ben Doney's pioneer cabin, artifacts pertaining to early medicine, logging and transportation in northern Arizona, and historic dolls and children's games. The Wool Festival, which is held at the museum in June, and the Independence Day Festival, on the Fourth of July, have live demonstrations.

Engine No. 12 outside the Pioneer Museum

A mile (1.6km) past the museum is the **Museum of ◀ Northern Arizona** (MNA; open daily 9am–5pm; admission fee). Founded by wealthy archeology enthusiast Dr Harold Colton and his wife Mary-Russell Ferrell Colton in 1928, the museum is the Northland's premier cultural institution. If you visit only one attraction in Flagstaff, this should be it. Rooms highlight the geology, biology, and culture of the Colorado Plateau, and the setting on the shady banks of the Rio de Flag is a perfect place for a picnic. At this museum, you'll learn more about the local Sinagua ('without water') Indians, identified by Colton, whose cliff dwellings and small pueblos can still be seen in this area.

The museum is the primary repository for artifacts from archaeological digs in northern Arizona. Revolving displays of prehistoric and contemporary Indian basketry, pottery, paintings, and kachina carvings are exhibited in the attractively laid-out museum. Throughout the summer and early fall, the museum holds a series of shows and marketplaces featuring work by local Navajo, Hopi, Zuni, and Paiutes. You can buy examples of their work at the shows and in the MNA's superb little onsite gift shop.

Day Hikes in Flagstaff

You can reach the San Francisco Peaks by continuing for 17 miles (27km) on Highway 180 then taking the road to the **Arizona Snowbowl** (open daily 9am–4pm), a popular ski resort. In summer, after the snow melts, the ski basin provides the main access into **Kachina Peaks Wilderness Area**, home to rare tundra flowers, elk, and Mexican owls. The four peaks are actually the remains of a single stratovolcano that blew its top about 400,000 years ago, piling up layers of lava, cinders, and ash to an elevation of 16,000ft (4,800m). The Inner Basin, on the north side, is the collapsed caldera of the volcano.

To reach the wilderness, take either the **Humphreys** or **Kachina Trails**. Kachina follows the lower slope and is

Humphreys Peak viewed from the Snowbowl ski area

the gentler of the two. The Humphreys Trail leads to the summit of the 12,643ft (3,854m) **Humphreys Peak**, Arizona's highest mountain. It is a long, steep, and challenging hike across the rocky tundra; be sure to dress warmly, no matter what time of year, because it is always cold and windy on top. An easier hike is possible through **Hart Prairie**, an historic meadow owned by the Nature Conservancy that offers hiking, overnight lodging in cabins, workshops, and retreats. The ski chair lift is open daily for fall leaf viewing in September and October.

   Mount Elden, on the east side of town off Route 66, is a popular local destination. The hike starts out in national forest and ascends the bare flanks of the mountain for good views of the Painted Desert and East Flag. At the foot of Mount Elden is partially excavated **Elden Pueblo**, a prehistoric Sinagua pueblo, sometimes open to visitors. During Archaeology Week in March, families may assist in digging at the pueblo.

Wupatki Pueblo and Sunset Crater

Evidence of Sinagua occupation can be found throughout the Flagstaff area. Two of the most interesting sites are

Wupatki National Monument and **Sunset Crater Volcano National Monument** (visitor center open daily 8am–5pm, pueblos sunrise to sunset; admission fee), off Highway 89, 22 miles (35km) northeast of Flagstaff. Sunset Crater Volcano, named by explorer John Wesley Powell, is one of the loveliest cinder cones in the San Francisco Volcanic Field. Eruptions formed the 1,000-ft (300-m) high cone starting in 1065 and ending in the 1200s. Sinagua farmers fled the eruptions but later returned in great numbers from the Verde Valley, attracted by soil made fertile by volcanic ash. Though the crater is now off limits to hikers due to erosion, you can walk around it on the mile (1.6-km) long **Lava Flow Trail**.

With views to the Painted Desert and Hopi Mesas to the east, and the San Francisco Mountains to the west, it's obvious that Wupatki's location close to the Little Colorado River was significant. Some of the excavated pueblos here are cleverly incorporated into natural boulders. The largest, **Wupatki Pueblo**, has more than 100 rooms that were built in phases, from the mid- to late 1130s through the early 1200s. Some of the masonry here resembles that of Chaco Canyon in present-day New Mexico, which was abandoned around the same time that construction began in Wupatki.

Even more intriguing is the large Hohokam Indian ball court, the northernmost such structure in Arizona, which may have been used by traders. Archaeologists theorize that Wupatki was an important trading pueblo on the northwest frontier of

Wupatki Pueblo

the southwest prehistoric world. Perhaps it hoped to emulate Chaco, whose residents were forced to establish new communities after Chaco fell in the mid-1100s.

Walnut Canyon National Monument

In the 13th century, cultural pressures and a prolonged drought led the Sinagua to move to **Walnut Canyon National Monument** (open daily 8am–5pm; admission fee), a few miles east of Flagstaff, south of Interstate 40. The people who lived here built snug cliff dwellings in sheltered limestone alcoves above a stream, farmed mesa-top fields, and constructed what appear to be forts, perhaps as defense against invaders. Descend the steep **Island Trail** to view the small, smoke-blackened rooms. The **Rim Walk** is a good place to view the remains of Sinagua fields and small check dams that helped to divert the water that irrigated them.

Cliff dwellings in Walnut Canyon

VERDE VALLEY AND SEDONA

Montezuma Castle National Monument (open daily 8am–7pm; admission fee), 50 miles (80km) south of Flagstaff, off Interstate 17, was built in the lush Verde Valley in the 12th century. Perched above a tributary of the Verde River, the small ruin is recessed into an alcove and may only be viewed from below. Although early explorers thought it the work of Aztecs, Sinagua refugees from Sunset Crater actually built the pueblo. They built it next to farmlands once occupied by Hohokam farmers from southern Arizona. A rare Hohokam pithouse is on view at **Montezuma Well**, 11 miles (18km) north of the monument.

Continue west through the fast-growing town of **Cottonwood** to **Tuzigoot National Monument** (open daily 8am–7pm; admission fee) to take a look at another defensive pueblo, this one up on a hill above the Verde River. Tuzigoot started out as a small pueblo in AD1000 and grew to 110 rooms in the 1200s. Year-round water and fertile soil in the Verde Valley brought many Sinagua immigrants from drought-ridden areas farther north, swelling the numbers of people in the valley and straining resources. Like Wupatki, the Verde Valley became an important crossroads for traders, and Tuzigoot was a central location used to house people and store food.

Apache Homeland

Tuzigoot was finally abandoned around 1425, when large numbers of Apache began using the area. Tonto Apache and Yavapai bands from the Colorado River intermarried in the Verde Valley and, after a long campaign against them by General Crook, were consolidated into the 550-acre (225-hectare) **Yavapai-Apache Reservation**.

Apache casinos in Camp Verde and Prescott have made the tribe the valley's largest employer, along with the historic

Verde Valley Railroad (tel: 800-293-7245), a former mine train that runs four-hour excursions daily from **Clarkdale** to **Perkinsville**. The train offers a unique opportunity to travel into **Sycamore Canyon Wilderness**, a 21-mile (34-km) long canyon with 700-ft (210-m) high cliff walls used by bald and golden eagles wintering by the river.

Jerome

The Verde Valley Railroad was financed by Senator William A. Clark, owner of the United Verde Mine in nearby **Jerome**, a scenic mine town perched atop 7,743-ft (2,360-m) **Mingus Mountain**. A former mining camp, which began life in 1876 and grew into one of the West's rowdiest mining towns, Jerome had 2,681 residents from all over the world in 1900. They mined $1 billion of copper, gold, silver, zinc, and lead during the mine's 77 years of operation. Artists moved in in

Gold King Mine ghost town, Jerome

the 1960s and rescued many of the Victorian 'Painted Ladies'. Today, many operate as galleries, bed-and-breakfasts, and restaurants, and the whole town is on the National Register of Historic Places.

Prescott

On the other side of Mingus Mountain, genteel **Prescott** was founded as Arizona's first state capital in 1864, after the first territorial governor John Goodwin and

Sharlot Hall Museum

other officials decided to build government buildings on Granite Creek, attracted by gold and grass for ranching. On Saturday nights, cowboys from surrounding cattle outfits blew into town and drank away their hard-earned cash in saloons on Whiskey Row, still the center of downtown. Prescott ho sts the 'world's oldest rodeo' every Fourth of July. A popular Cowboy Poets' Gathering attracts bards of the open range to town every August.

Stop at the **Sharlot Hall Museum** (open Mon–Sat 10am– 5pm, Sun 1–5pm; admission fee), housed in the former Governor's Mansion and 11 other buildings to learn more about Prescott. The museum was founded in 1928 by erstwhile territorial historian Sharlot Hall, the first woman to be inducted into Arizona's Hall of Fame. Hall singlehandedly ran her family's ranch in the Prescott area and explored remote areas on horseback. Her writings extolling the beauty of northern Arizona's little-known Arizona Strip helped persuade Congress to include the area when Arizona won statehood in 1912.

Sedona

Return to Flagstaff on Highway 89A via **Sedona** and **Oak Creek**, which together make up Arizona's world-famous **Red Rock Country**. Many people find themselves inexorably drawn to the mesmerizing (and some say, unearthly) beauty of Sedona, with its fancifully eroded redrock buttes, year round Oak Creek, and forested trails leading directly from town into the surrounding 44,000-acre (17,800-hectare) **Red Rock-Secret Mountain Wilderness**.

High-end resorts and multimillion-dollar homes stuccoed in post-modern desert hues of terracotta, buckskin, and verdigris sprawl along Highway 89A, interspersed with fashionable restaurants, tour companies, New Age healing centers, and shops selling overpriced T-shirts infused with the healing properties of sacred Sedona mud. Beyond the commercial corridor, though, lies a different Sedona: one

Rock pool in Oak Creek Canyon

where you can still look up at a robin's-egg blue sky curving above red cliffs and see red-tailed hawks soaring. Climb up to Sinagua Indian ruins at **Palatki** and **Honanki** and hike and camp in the Coconino National Forest.

The area's loveliest hike is the 3-mile (5-km) **West Fork of Oak Creek Trail**, north of Sedona in **Oak Creek Canyon**, the spectacular 3,000-ft (900-m)-deep gash in the mountains carved by Oak Creek. Zane Grey was inspired by this deep canyon to write his classic *Call of the Canyon*; it retains the historic orchards, ranches, rustic cabins, and wilderness feel of a time gone by. On hot summer days, 55-acre (22-hectare) **Slide Rock State Park** (open daily 9am–8pm) is one of the most popular places in the Northland. The natural rock chute into the creek is the perfect cool-off spot before driving back to Flagstaff.

NAVAJO AND HOPI COUNTRY

For many people, a visit to the Navajo and Hopi Reservations, east of Flagstaff, is the highlight of their trip to northern Arizona. Time seems to stand still in this epic landscape, whose stone landmarks and secret canyons are sacred to the people who have called this home for many centuries.

The 29,817-sq mile (77,226-sq km) **Navajo Nation** is the largest Indian reservation in the country. The Western Navajo reservation includes many of Arizona's most interesting parks: Monument Valley, Navajo National Monument, Canyon de Chelly, Petrified Forest, and Hubbell Trading Post. Paved roads lead to all of them, and you could easily spend a week traveling around the reservation.

In order to represent the 300,000 *Dineh*, as the people call themselves, communities are divided into 110 'chapters', or local councils, which send 88 delegates to speak for them at the tribal council at the 1868 tribal headquarters in **Window Rock**, near the Arizona–New Mexico border. Chapter houses

serve as community centers for remote communities, a place where people can speak to their representatives, socialize with fellow residents, pick up their mail, and receive services. If you get lost on backroads, stop at a chapter house. You'll nearly always find someone who speaks enough English to point you back to the main road.

Monument Valley

Monument Valley Navajo Tribal Park (open daily except Christmas Day 8am–7pm; admission fee), the crown jewel in the Navajo tribal park system, tops the list of must-see sights on the Big Rez. This iconic western landscape is one

Monument Valley

of several scenic and historic areas set aside as tribal parks in the 1950s to protect Navajo lands that were being exploited for coal, oil, gas, uranium, and other natural resources that have enriched the tribe. It is managed by a full onsite staff and administered from Window Rock. For more information contact **Navajo Parks and Recreation** (tel: 928-871-6647).

To reach Monument Valley, drive north on Highway 89 and turn east onto Highway 160, passing through **Tuba City**. When you reach **Kayenta,** head north 20 miles (32km) on Highway 163 to the park. The only lodging inside the park is the 100-site **Mittens Campground**. Though basic, it's the best place to see the sunrise behind the carved de Shay sandstone formations. Motel rooms are available at historic **Gouldings Lodge**, on the other side of Highway 160, along with a gas station, a supermarket, an ATM machine, and restaurants.

Gouldings includes the original 1923 trading post built by trader Harry Goulding and his wife 'Mike', now a small museum filled with memorabilia. Goulding was responsible for bringing Hollywood film director John Ford to Monument Valley in the 1930s. Throughout the Forties, Ford used the famous valley as the backdrop for many of his movies, including *Stagecoach, She Wore a Yellow Ribbon, The Searchers, Sergeant Rutledge*, and *Cheyenne Autumn*. The cabin used by John Wayne, Ford's favorite leading actor, can be seen behind the trading post.

A number of Navajo families live inside park boundaries, on traditional homesteads usually consisting of a frame house, a hogan (log and earth hut), a shady *ramada* (shelter), a nearby sweat lodge, and livestock corrals for sheep, goats, and horses. Many local Navajos are licensed with the tribe to offer horseback and Jeep tours of their homeland. Some outside tour companies also operate inside the park. These companies are usually operated by Anglos and offer less of an opportunity to meet Navajos. Tours with a Navajo guide can

The Three Sisters, encountered on the scenic drive

be arranged at the kiosk in front of the visitor center or at booths along the entrance road. Fees (cash only) are reasonable, but be sure to tip your guide and any Navajos who pose for photographs.

For most, this seasonal income is their primary means of support. Note: off-road hiking, biking, camping, horseback riding, and four-wheel driving are only permitted with a registered Navajo guide.

Allow at least two hours to tour the 17-mile (27-km), unpaved scenic drive into the valley. The dusty, rutted road is drivable by passenger cars but becomes impassable after rain. Inquire before setting out, and take plenty of food and water. There are no services along the tour route. A tour booklet available at the visitor center identifies 11 scenic overlooks along the drive, including **John Ford Point**, the vista instantly recognizable from Ford's Westerns. **Sand Springs**, the valley's only water source, offers glimpses of a hogan, corrals, sheep, goats, and local residents dressed in traditional velvet clothing.

The impressively sited Betatakin

Navajo National Monument

Navajos live next to the prehistoric dwellings and granaries of Pueblo people, known to the Navajo as *Anasazi*, meaning 'enemy ancestors' or 'those who came before'. A side tour in Monument Valley will take you into **Mystery Valley** to view small Anasazi pueblos, but to see the most beautifully preserved of the late-period Kayenta Anasazi cliff dwellings, don't miss little-known **Navajo National Monument** (open daily; admission free), 28 miles (45km) west of Kayenta. From the small visitor center, the ½-mile (1-km) **Sandal Trail** leads to an overlook above **Betatakin** (Navajo for 'ledge house'), a simply spectacular 135-room pueblo built in AD1250 in a 450-ft (135-m) high alcove above Tsegi Canyon. Scheduled 5-mile (8-km) hikes to Betatakin, led by a ranger, are offered each morning in summer and are limited to 25 hikers. It's first come, first served. The best way to ensure a spot on the tour is to camp in the large free campground, one of the prettiest spots around.

Canyon de Chelly

Canyon de Chelly National Monument

The Navajo word *tsegi* means 'rock canyon'. Tsegi Canyon was carved by the Rio de Chelly ('de-shay'), a corruption of tsegi, through the Defiance Plateau, where it has created a 1,000-ft (300-m) deep canyon that rivals the Grand Canyon for beauty and history. The best place to view this canyon is from the **Canyon de Chelly National Monument** (open daily; admission free) off Highway 191, south of Highway 160. The park is next to **Chinle**, which has gas, food, and lodging.

Accommodations inside the park is at **Thunderbird Lodge**, a 1902 trading post that offers motel rooms, a cafeteria, rugs made by local artisans, and tours into the sandy-bottomed canyon in large open-air vehicles. You can also hire a Navajo tour guide to ride with you in your own high-clearance, four-wheel-drive vehicle. The only hiking access is the 2-mile (3-km) **White House Ruin Trail**, which leads to one of more than 700 Anasazi ruins in the canyon built between the 11th and 13th centuries. You will frequently meet Navajos going in and out of the canyon on this trail. Many grow corn and other crops in the canyon seasonally, and return to the rim to graze livestock during the school year.

The 35-mile (56-km) long **South** and **North Rim Drives** offer scenic overlooks of ruins in the main canyon and its equally pretty neighbor **Canyon del Muerto**. The Anasazi who built these cliff dwellings moved to the Hopi Mesas during the Great Drought of 1276–99, and their Hopi descendants returned to farm and plant peach trees obtained from the Spanish after 1540. Navajos hid out here from the Spanish in the 1700s. In 1805, 115 men, women, and children were murdered by Spanish soldiers in **Massacre Cave** in Canyon del Muerto.

The Navajo were equally persecuted during the early American period. On 9 September 1849, tribal leaders signed a peace treaty acknowledging American rule on the south rim of Canyon de Chelly. The fragile treaty degenerated into war, subjugation, and incarceration in 1864, when Lt Kit Carson used a 'scorched earth' policy in Canyon de Chelly and other Navajo strongholds to destroy Navajo culture. Navajos who surrendered were forced to walk to Fort Sumner in eastern New Mexico, where thousands died of starvation, disease, and servitude. In 1868, survivors were allowed to return to a newly created reservation on the Defiance Plateau.

Hubbell Trading Post

During their four years of captivity at the US Army

> Unlike Hopi dances, Navajo ceremonials are not usually performed in public. They are family affairs conducted in the privacy of a hogan, over several days. The aim is to bring individuals back into harmony with the Beauty Path – a way of living in the world given to the Navajo in mythic times by First Man and First Woman.

post at Fort Sumner, Navajo people survived by developing a taste for Anglo foods like canned peaches, Arbuckle coffee, and white Bluebird flour. The traditional Navajo women's dress of velveteen or calico tiered skirt and blouse was an adaptation of the Mother Hubbard dresses worn by Army wives. In the 1870s, traders like Lorenzo Hubbell set up trading posts selling these goods in return for woven rugs, silver jewelry, baskets, and other arts and crafts that could be sold to markets back east. **Hubbell Trading Post National Historic Site** (open daily; admission free), now a national historic site west of Ganado, is a well-preserved post. Hubbell was a good friend to the Navajo, helping them to improve their arts and crafts for sale, extending credit, and acting as intermediary in disputes between the Navajo and the government. Visitors may tour the historic Hubbell home, which is chock-full of memorabilia.

Light show in the Painted Desert

Petrified Forest National Park

The area between Flagstaff and Ganado is known as the **Painted Desert**, for the shifting pastel hues found in the Chinle Formation, a crumbly rock formation that appeared 200 million years ago, when the region was populated by dinosaurs among tall trees and huge ferns. Trees that fell into swamps were buried by ash during eruptions from nearby volcanoes. Their forms were perfectly preserved, as silicates replaced their woody cells, creating jasper and other gemstones. You can see many examples of fossilized wood at the minimally developed **Petrified Forest National Park** (open daily 7.30am–5pm; admission free), near **Holbrook**. A scenic drive takes you along

Ancient tree trunk in the Petrified Forest National Park

the Rio Puerco to a petroglyph site and nearby **Agate House**, which was built using fossilized wood.

Prehistoric Indians were also responsible for the 300 partially excavated ruins at **Homolovi Ruins State Park** (open daily 9am–5pm; admission free) near the railroad town of **Winslow**. There is a campground here and scenic drives to view petroglyphs that show a blend of Ancestral Pueblo and Mogollon cultural influences.

The Mogollon People

The Mogollon lived in the highlands of southwestern New Mexico in the early Christian era and were the first to learn pottery making, farming, and stone pueblo building from their Mexican neighbors. **Casa Malpais**, in the scenic White Mountains, is the most accessible of several Mogollon ruins in northeastern Arizona, where the Mogollon merged with their northern neighbors, the Ancestral Pueblo, in the 11th century.

Tours leave daily from the **Casa Malpais Museum and Visitor Center** (open daily 9am–5pm; admission fee) on

Main Street in **Springerville,** one of a handful of Mormon ranching towns founded in the 1870s. Guides take you round the large hilltop pueblo, which was occupied by 300 people and has an unusual Great Kiva in the rectangular shape typical of Mogollon ceremonial rooms.

The pueblo is made from lava rock, or *malpais* stone, which came from the nearby White Mountain Volcanic Field. **Baldy Peak**, the highest mountain, is sacred to the **White Mountain Apache**, whose reservation adjoins the mountain towns of **Pine Top/Lakeside.** You can hunt, fish, hike, camp, and enjoy numerous outdoor pursuits on the reservation and adjoining White Mountain lands. The area is a favorite with Phoenix and Tucson residents in summer.

Greer

One of the most popular destinations in the White Mountains is Greer, a tiny hamlet at the headwaters of the Little Colorado River with many rustic cabins, resorts, and trails. Founded by Molly and John Butler and other Mormon homesteaders in 1879, the town did well selling meat, grain, and other necessities to army forts in the area charged with subduing the Apache.

In 1914, explorer, naturalist, and writer James Willard Schultz, moved to a cabin in Greer. While there, he wrote *In the Great Apache Forest: The Story of a Lone Boy Scout,* a tale inspired by the World War I adventures of Molly Butler's children, George and Hannah Crosby. Schultz had lived among the Blackfoot tribe in Montana and married a Blackfoot woman. His son Hart Merriam, known as Lone Wolf, a popular American Indian artist, joined his father at the cabin he called *Apuni Oyis* (Butterfly Lodge). Lone Wolf inherited the cabin and lived there on and off until his death in 1970. Today the home is on the National Register of Historic Places and is now a museum (open summer weekends only; admission free).

The airport at Gouldings, Monument Valley

Air Tours
Fixed-wing and helicopter tours of the Grand Canyon region take off daily from Grand Canyon Airport in Tusayan. **Papillon Grand Canyon Helicopters** (tel: 800-528-2418; <www.papillon.com>) has North Canyon and West Canyon flights originating at Grand Canyon Airport and all-day coach/flight tours operating from Flagstaff, Sedona, and Scottsdale/Phoenix.

Mule Rides
Grand Canyon's famous mule rides give visitors a chance to get below the canyon rim without the difficult hike. But you need to be able to speak English, weigh under 200lbs (88kg), be over 4ft 7in (1.4m) tall, not pregnant, unaffected by vertigo, willing to follow your wrangler's instructions, and have sufficient muscular control to stay on your mount for long hours in an exposed environment.

Mule rides range from day trips to Plateau Point and two- and three-day trips, with stays at Phantom Ranch in the Inner Canyon. On the South Rim, mule strings led by a seasoned wrangler leave each morning from the Mule Corrals near Bright Angel Lodge and head down Bright Angel Trail. Meals and snacks are included; lodging and other meals at Phantom Ranch are additional. Book well ahead of time. On the North Rim, half- and one-day mule rides take you down the North Kaibab Trail. Reserve at **Grand Canyon Trail Rides** desk (tel: 435-679-8665) in Grand Canyon Lodge. Daily rides are usually available on this less-visited rim.

Riding through Monument Valley

Apache Stables (closed in winter, tel: 928-638-2631) in Tusayan offers one-, two-, and four-hour rides and twilight campfire and wagon rides into the Coconino National Forest. A number of families on the Navajo reservation run horseback rides into the backcountry. Family outfits like the Blacks in **Monument Valley** have roadside stands on the entrance route where you can enjoy a ride into the park.

Historic Train Rides

The classic way to arrive at the South Rim is on the historic steam train run by **Grand Canyon Railway** (tel:

800-THE-TRAIN) in Williams. Locomotives pulling refurbished Pullman cars leave at 10am and arrive at the 1901 Railway Depot in the center of Grand Canyon Village at 12.15pm. You can take the train one way and return the same day at 3.30pm, or stay overnight at the Canyon.

Grand Canyon Railway has its own pleasant trackside **Grand Canyon Railway Lodge** in Williams, with a huge antique Victorian bar imported from an old London pub; a great place to relax for a while and have a drink and a snack after a day of sightseeing.

**Verde River Canyon
Excursion Train**

Train visitors can get the most out of the three-hour layover at the canyon by doing a guide-narrated Harvey coach tour of Grand Canyon Village or West Rim Drive. The one-and-a-half-hour village **Freedom Tour** includes a box lunch, and the two-and-a-half-hour **Grand Tour** includes buffet lunch at Maswik Lodge, thus solving the perennial problem of long lunch lines at the South Rim.

Just as delightful is the historic train ride into the Sycamore Canyon Wilderness on the **Verde River Canyon Excursion Train** (tel: 800-293-7245), between the former mining towns of Clarkdale to Perkinsville. The gaily painted scenic train provides a great family outing into a deep canyon carved by the Verde River. This is an excellent way to see the abundant wildlife of the region, including many raptors that use the cliffs as their staging areas for hunting.

Merriam's Life Zones

In the 1800s, naturalist C. Hart Merriam noted that elevation changes within a single region allowed a range of wildlife to live there that would normally only be found by crossing the United States from Mexico (lowest) to Canada (highest). The 6,000-ft (1,800-m) elevation difference accounts for three different life zones, as Merriam called them, at the Grand Canyon.

The Rim Country: Plants and animals of the **Transition** (7,000–8,250ft/2,100–2,475m) and **Upper Sonoran** (3,500–7,000ft/1,050–2,100m) zones live along canyon rims. The signature plants of the Upper Sonoran Zone are pinyon and juniper trees, stunted by heat and aridity, and interspersed with woody cliffrose, blackbrush, and sagebrush and prickly pear cactus. Away from the rim, greater elevation and more moisture allows swaying ponderosa pine to form airy forests in the Transition zone, along with Gambel oak and eye-catching wildflowers, such as Indian paintbrush, lupine, woolly mullein, sunflowers, orange globemallow, and other wildflowers. Aberts and Kaibab squirrels live on opposite rims, separated by the canyon. Watch for mule deer and coyotes at dusk.

Inner Gorge: Desert abuts a riparian environment along the Colorado River, a good place to see blue herons and eagles in winter. Desert yucca thrives across from thirsty pink-tipped tamarisk, or saltcedar, an invader that crowds out natural willows and cottonwood trees. Flycatchers, Bell's vireo, white-breasted nuthatch, endangered southwest willow flycatchers, and other songbirds use the trees as cover. Water seeping through sandstone nurtures 'hanging gardens' of colorful columbines, monkeyflower, and maidenhair fern. In the colder waters emerging from Lake Powell, sport fish like rainbow trout are thriving – a big draw for eagles – while native warm-water species like humpback chub, razorback sucker, and Colorado squawfish are now endangered.

OUTDOOR SPORTS

Grand Canyon and nearby
towns are filled with outdoors
enthusiasts who can never get
enough hiking, river-running,
winter skiing, marathon running, and other sports. For
those living in Flagstaff or
Sedona, it's understandable:
both towns are surrounded
by the Coconino National
Forest, and trails start from
outside your door.

On the Bright Angel Trail

Hiking

Hiking is available year round in the Northland. Cool, high-
country forest walks in the San Francisco Peaks or the
White Mountains offer an escape from summer heat. In
winter, 4,000-ft (1,200-m) elevation Sedona and Oak
Creek's trailheads and campgrounds come into their own.
All are clean and beautifully maintained through funds from
the Sedona Red Rock Pass, an inexpensive and easily available visitor permit.

Both rims of the Grand Canyon offer easy day hikes,
from spring to fall; the South Rim trail can get icy in winter, so watch your step near the canyon edge. For most people, the South and North Kaibab, Bright Angel, and
Hualapai Hilltop trails into the inner canyon are too long
and steep, and the dry summer heat prevents descent into the
canyon itself. Two shorter below-the-rim day hikes at the
South Rim are worth considering, though. Eight-mile (13-km)
Hermit Trail, at the end of West Rim Drive, follows a pretty
miners' route to Dripping Springs, and **Cedar Ridge** on the

South Kaibab Trail, although unshaded, offers glimpses of the inner canyon.

There are more options for short forested hikes on the North Rim. The 3-mile (5-km) **Transept Trail**, which follows a forest trail between the lodge and campground, is perfect for the whole family.

River-running

For many of the 22,000 people a year who pay to raft the Colorado River each year, a whitewater trip through the Grand Canyon is the realization of a lifelong dream. To run the whole river, from Lees Ferry on the east to Diamond Creek on the west, is a two- to three-week undertaking, depending on whether the company uses motorized rubber rafts or oar-powered rafts and wooden dories, similar to John Wesley Powell's 1869 *Emma Dean*. Concessionaires offer

Negotiating the Lava Falls in the western Grand Canyon

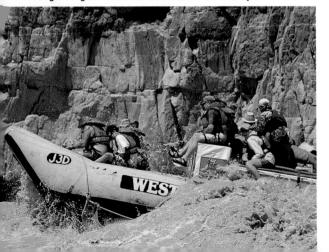

experienced and entertaining guides, plenty of thrilling rides on whitewater rapids, gourmet meals, campfire stories, and the camaraderie of the river – an experience that will stay with you for ever.

You can also get a flavor of the river by doing a short flat-water trip. **Wilderness River Adventures** (tel: 800-528-6154) runs half-day family floats from the put-in below Glen Canyon Dam to Lees Ferry. All-day trips originating at Diamond Creek are offered by **Hualapai River Runners** (tel: 928-645-3279) in the western end of the canyon.

Lake Boating

The most popular destination for water sports is **Lake Powell**, the reservoir backed up by Glen Canyon Dam. Several marinas rent sea kayaks, houseboats, and large cabin cruisers. Many people tow their own boats and jet skis to the lake to water-ski and swim. Most Arizonans put in at **Wahweap Marina**, next to Page, which has full services. The quieter Utah side at **Bullfrog Marina** and **Hite Crossing** is much more remote. A small car ferry operates from Bullfrog to Hite, a fun way to get out on the water. Camping is available on sandy beaches and at developed campgrounds adjoining the lake.

Rafting the San Juan

North of Monument Valley, five-day and shorter float trips on the **San Juan River** are popular with local river enthusiasts. River trips leave from **Bluff** or **Mexican Hat, Utah**, and take out just before the San Juan dies in Lake Powell. Most of the time, you're simply drifting, kayaking, and enjoying the sights of pueblo ruins, waterfalls, and geological landmarks carved out of creamy Cedar Mesa Sandstone. **Recapture Lodge**, in Mexican Hat, has rooms, food, and daily river trips.

Skiing

North of Flagstaff, **Arizona Snowbowl** has downhill skiing that attracts skiiers from throughout Arizona. A nearby **Nordic Ski Center**, with groomed trails, offers daily cross-country ski lessons and rentals. You can ski into the Kaibab National Forest surrounding the North Rim of the Grand Canyon when it is closed by snow between November and May. Jacob Lake Inn is open year round, but all services in the park are closed.

Bryce Canyon in the snow

To the north, in Utah, **Bryce Canyon National Park** is another great destination for snowshoers and cross-country skiers, open throughout the winter for amazing views of eroded pinnacles and other formations. Farther south, in the White Mountains, the Apache operate **Sunrise Ski Resort** surrounding Mount Baldy, near **Hondah**. You'll find ice fishing, cross-country skiing, tobogganing, and snowshoeing in the Apache-Sitgreaves National Forest near the Arizona-New Mexico border.

CHILDREN'S ACTIVITIES

National park vacations are a time-honored American family tradition. They're cheap, fun, filled with attractions, and outdoor activities that will help lively youngsters let off steam. Most kids do not appreciate long hours doing scenic drives through beautiful landscapes. You're better off choosing one park or town as your base (e.g. Tusayan, Flagstaff) and doing short drives to destinations where kids can hike, swim, ride a bike, run around, play ball, and camp. Museums and visitor centers have many hands-on educational activities, including learning to grind corn, make an Archaic atlatl spear thrower or arrowhead, dig for artifacts with archaeologists, identify plants on a ranger walk, or climb inside a reconstructed pueblo. Park and museum stores have a good range of educational, activity, and story books on the region aimed at kids.

Ask at Canyon View Information Plaza in Grand Canyon National Park about the **Junior Ranger** program, where kids complete a booklet of activities and receive a badge at the park. Invent some park-specific games. One easy one is **Park I-SPY**, using words like Colorado River, fossils, dinosaur tracks, pueblo ruins, park ranger, thunderbird, ponderosa pine, aspen, Kaibab or Aberts squirrel, and lodge.

The whole family will enjoy visiting the **Mule Corrals** at 8am to see the mules being saddled up for rides into the canyon. In Tusayan, kids can swim in the only indoor pool in the area at the Grand Hotel, play video games in the Family Fun Center across the street, do an easy horseback ride in the forest, watch an IMAX movie, eat some fast food, and even surf the internet at a cyber cafe.

SHOPPING

Several stores at the South Rim sell books, posters, postcards, and unique gifts, from soft toys to CDs, DVDs, videos, and clothing. **Books and More** in Canyon View Information Plaza is run by **Grand Canyon Association**. All profits go to support the park. You'll also find small retail stores at Bright Angel Lodge, Desert View, El Tovar, Hermit's Rest, Hopi House, Kolb Studio, Lookout Studio, Maswik Lodge, Tusayan Museum, Verkamp's Curios,

Indian crafts at the Hopi House

Yavapai Observation Station, and Yavapai Curio Shop.

Groceries, ice, and snacks, are sold at general stores in Grand Canyon Village, Desert View, and Tusayan. **Hopi House, Verkamp's Curios**, and **Desert View Watchtower** specialize in Indian-made items, including beautiful woven Navajo rugs and collectable folk art, carved Hopi kachina dolls, Paiute baskets, beaded Apache keyrings, Indian jewelry, and pottery made by Pueblos as well as Navajo artists. In Flagstaff, the little gift shop at the **Museum of Northern Arizona** has an excellent selection of items, many culled from the museum's juried art shows by Navajo, Hopi, Zuni, and Paiute artisans. **Puchteca Gallery**, on San Francisco Street, is another good bet for traditional and contemporary Indian art.

Trading Posts

Historic trading posts are found throughout the area. The 1878 **Hubbell Trading Post**, near Ganado, is an experience in itself. Its wonderful rug room is filled to the rafters with Ganado, Klagetoh, Teec Nos Pos, Crystal, Chinle, Wide Ruins, Two Grey Hills, and Burntwater style rugs associated with different areas of the Navajo reservation. Also look for unusual patterns such as storm, twill, tapestry, and mosaic. Monument Valley weavers often create pictorial rugs featuring Yei or Yeibichei dancers and scenes from daily Navajo life.

Turquoise stone, sacred to southwest Indians, is shaped into disks *(heishi)*, nuggets, pendants, and other forms and set into silver to make heavy squash blossom and other styles of necklace, bracelets, earrings, watch bands, and belt buckles. In the 1800s, silver coins from the US government were sewn onto clothing and became a Navajo's personal wealth, snipped off and used for purchases or melted down to make silver jewelry. Concha belts, originally made from coins and now made from stamped silver, harken back to that time.

Ceremonial baskets are traditionally woven by Navajos and Southern Paiutes on the Shonto Plateau area, just south of Lake Powell. Baskets by award-winning basketmaker Mary Black can be found just north of Monument Valley, at **Blue Mountain Trading Post** in Blanding and **Twin Rocks Trading Post** in Bluff. Throughout the Navajo and Hopi reservations, you can purchase direct from artisans, either at their home studios or at roadside booths – a great way to meet and learn about the local cultures.

Hubbell Trading Post

If it's contemporary art you crave, your best bet is to head to Sedona's famous **Tlaquepaque Market**, a Mexican-style *mercado* in uptown Sedona filled with shops, galleries, and restaurants. The work here includes classic Western art, watercolors and pastel drawings of southwest scenes, innovative ceramics, and oversized sculptures.

Calendar of Events

January: Flagstaff WinterFest celebrates winter snow, with ice carving, sleigh riding, dog sledding, and other snow sports.

April: Flagstaff's popular annual Book Festival brings world-famous writers to venues around town for readings and panel discussions.

July: Territorial Days and Rodeo in Prescott includes a rodeo, a Cowboy Poetry Gathering, and festivities at Sharlot Hall Museum. The Niman, or Hopi Home Dance, celebrates the return of the *katsinas,* or spirits, to their winter home on the San Francisco Peaks after blessing the crops and bringing the rain. Juried Hopi, Navajo, and Pai Marketplaces are held on weekends at Museum of Northern Arizona in Flagstaff.

August: The World's Oldest Continuous Rodeo takes place in Payson. Flagstaff's Festival in the Pines brings families to Fort Tuthill County Fairgrounds for music, dancing, food booths, and face painting.

September: Grand Canyon Chamber Music Association brings world-class musicians to the South Rim's lovely Shrine of the Ages auditorium for concerts highlighted by late-season thunderstorms on the rim. Flag's weeklong Festival of Science includes lectures and hands-on family events at Lowell Observatory, Museum of Northern Arizona, and Northern Arizona University and the rare opportunity to help excavate city-owned Elden Pueblo with the resident archaeologist.

October: Sedona Arts Festival celebrates art in Red Rock Country with booths, events, and shows.

November: Flagstaff's WorldFest International Film Festival brings film lovers to the Northland for movie premieres.

EATING OUT

Don't get your hopes up for gourmet dining in northern Arizona. This is rural ranch country. Folks get up at dawn to beat the heat, many do a full workday outside, and go to bed early. Meals are large and eaten early in the day and are usually accompanied by thin watery brewed coffee or iced tea. Beer is more common than wine, and many people drink milk or milkshakes. Burgers, barbecue, potpies, and other variations on meat and potatoes are the norm, followed by fresh-baked pies filled with home-canned fruits.

Spanish Spice

Early Spanish colonists introduced the concept of ranching and many new foods unknown to the native people of North America: potatoes, tomatoes, and hot chili peppers from Central and Southern America; avocados, grapes, and melons; and foods from Europe, such as orchard fruits and wheat. But while the Apache, Navajo, and Hopi in Arizona adopted horses, fruit growing, and *hornos* (beehive ovens), they never submitted to Spanish rule and were only later exposed to these foods, when the territory passed to Mexican rule in 1821.

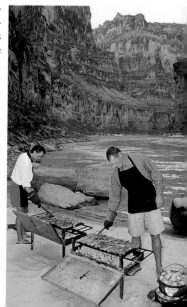

Barbecue at the river

Mexican Influences

Much of the food you're likely to run into as you travel reflects Arizona's Mexican and ranching past. In southern Arizona, this means lots of *ranchero* meat dishes from Sonora, the huge province just over the border where cattle is king. Favorite Sonoran delicacies are *carne seca* (sun-dried beef simmered with onions and peppers), *chile colorado* (red chili), and *chile verde* (green chili), which were developed in the kitchens of Spanish land-grant ranches along the border.

In popular new-wave Sonoran restaurants, you'll often find a changing daily chalkboard of light, flavorful Mexican dishes that feature huge shrimp and other seafood caught in the Gulf of California, just two hours southwest of Tucson. Warm home-made tortillas filled with flash-grilled chicken, fish, fresh vegetables, and fresh-chopped salsas of tomatoes, onions, chilis, coriander, avocado, and other seasonings have long been a feature of roadside grills in Mexico. Fish tacos and other cheap Baja, California-type fare can be found in college towns and have become popular as a cheap, healthy alternative to heavier Mexican fare.

The spicy peppers used in southwest cooking are known as *chile* in New Mexico, the correct Spanish spelling. Elsewhere, the Americanized spelling of *chili* is used. The spicy Texan meat-and-beans dish is correctly known as *chili con carne* (chili with meat) but is more usually just called *chili*. Before you order, ask exactly what you're getting.

Mexican Food

Americanized Mexican fare has long meant huge single and combination *platos* (dishes). All rely on corn and flour tortillas filled with meat, fish, vegetables, and cheese, covered in sauces and accompanied by refried beans, rice pilaf, shredded lettuce, avocado, sour

Guacamole and salsa

cream, and salsa. For breakfast, choose rolled-flour tortilla *burritos* (little donkeys) with scrambled eggs, potatoes, and chili. A more substantial breakfast dish is *huevos rancheros*, a piping-hot concoction of corn tortillas, topped with fried eggs, cheese, salsa, and refried beans.

Oven-baked *enchiladas* have the consistency of lasagna and can be filled with meat, spinach, or cheese, then topped with red sauce and cheese. Deep-fried *chimichangas, flautas, chalupas, tacos,* and *tacitos,* can be snacks or full meals. *Fajitas,* a Texan dish consisting of skirt steak, peppers, and onions with spices, is served in a hot, sizzling cast-iron frying pan and scooped up in warm flour tortillas. Harder to find in northern Arizona is the ancient Aztec dish of *tamales,* which consists of corn-masa dough filled with meat and vegetables and steamed in a corn husk. And if a restaurant specializes in *chile rellenos,* a rich combination of mild bellpeppers filled with cheese, battered, and deep fried, it's advisable to try one. Done well, they're a treat.

Happy Hour

Happy hour (usually between 4 and 7pm) is a good time to try Mexican appetizers *(antojitos)*. As soon as you sit down, most restaurants will serve you fresh fried tortilla chips with a chopped salsa of red tomatoes, onions, chilis, and cilantro (coriander). There are numerous versions of salsa, which has become America's favorite condiment. It's traditional in Mexico to blend different types of fire-roasted chili, straight from a hot grill, in a blender to make a fresh, puréed red salsa *(salsa roja)*. *Salsa verde* has a tangy flavor that comes from its use of green *tomatillos,* a husked fruit unrelated to tomatoes.

The spiced, mashed avocado dip of *guacamole* is a special treat and usually costs extra. It is often included as part of the popular sports bar appetizer known as *nachos* (tortilla chips covered in ground beef, melted cheese, refried beans, sour cream, olives, and salsa). Accompanied by an ice-cold Mexican beer or frozen Margarita (tequila, lime juice, and triple sec), this will only set you back a few bucks and can be shared among a whole table.

Cowboy Cuisine

Northern Arizona has been less influenced by Mexican cuisine than the border country. In the 1800s, it was settled by pioneer Anglo ranchers, many of whom favored meat-and-

---

The Three Sisters

Traditional southwest cuisine uses the Three Sisters – corn, beans, and squash. Pueblos developed different varieties of corn that would grow under dry, high-elevation growing conditions. Blue and red corn have been developed for ceremonies as well as eating. You can sample blue corn pancakes and a paper-thin ceremonial flatbread called *piki* at the Hopi Cultural Center restaurant on Second Mesa.

potatoes cuisine. On round-ups, the trail boss would roll a large chuckwagon to camp, and a designated 'cookie' would then prepare campfire staples like bacon and eggs at breakfast; steak, and barbecued ribs at dinner, accompanied by fresh cornbread and warm biscuits (similar to a British scone), baked potatoes, cole slaw, and slow-cooked baked beans.

Cornbread

Desserts on the range were rare. Homesteads that grew their own fruit in orchards watered by neighboring streams often baked extra pies for travelers who would show up at their door, hungry. Mormon homesteads in the Arizona Strip were famous for their fruit orchards and pies in the 1800s. A cookbook of pioneer recipes is published by **Zion Natural History Association** and available in the gift shop at Pipe Spring National Monument.

Dutch-oven Cooking

Out west, dutch-oven cooking has never really gone out of fashion, whether done over a campfire or campstove. In this one large cast-iron pot, you can make everything from stews and Texas-style meat chili to cakes and breads, as long as you have a little know-how. On Colorado River trips, you'll marvel over the delicious food cooked in a dutch oven by talented backcountry chefs. The descendants of pioneer

The one Indian staple you are likely to find in Indian Country, is fry-bread, traditionally made from white flour, deep fried, and served with powdered sugar. It is the foundation for Navajo tacos, an Indian version of the Mexican favorite with bean, ground beef or mutton, salsa, and all the fixings. This Indian fast food is popular at Indian pow wows, fairs, and ceremonials.

families also treasure the old-fashioned recipes handed down from thrifty relatives and will often break them out for guests. Many Mormon families like to camp out and hold huge family reunions around Pioneer Day (24 July), which commemorates the arrival of the Mormons in Salt Lake City led by Brigham Young in 1857.

Nouvelle Western

In recent years, chefs in Arizona's swankier resorts have begun to experiment with a bolder style of cooking dubbed 'Nouvelle Western'. It's hardly new, though. Dishes tend to feature traditional American Indian foods such as elk, rabbit, venison, free-range chicken, grass-fed beef, and wild salmon accompanied by wild rice, corn, squash, southwest pinyon nuts, prickly pear cactus pads and fruits, wild desert greens, and heritage varieties of organic produce. At its best, this is food that says it all about community and culture. Homegrown organic foods can be found at farmers' markets in Flagstaff and Sedona.

WHERE TO EAT

Northern Arizonans like to eat out, but given the great distances in the mountains, they are often hard-up for choice. The greatest selection of eateries can be found at or near places frequented by tourists and college students, or commercial centers, such as Flagstaff, Window Rock, and Payson, used by local residents.

Meal Times

It's common to eat breakfast before 8am and break for lunch at noon. Westerners tend to eat dinner between 5 and 7pm. If you're willing to eat later, then you can often get into the most popular restaurants without booking, especially at the Grand Canyon.

Grand Canyon Dining

The South Rim has soda fountains and cafeterias where you can get hot dogs, burgers, sandwiches, pastries, fresh fruit, ice cream, and other quick meals. Some of the best fast food can be found in the deli in the Marketplace in Market Plaza. Try the meat chili and soups in a sourdough bread bowl for an unusual lunch. You can get good Seattle's Best coffee here.

It's essential to make reservations for dinner. At the South Rim, the dark-paneled **El Tovar Hotel** dining room is the place for an elegant meal, preferably at sunset, when the colors of the canyon a few feet from the large picture window are most glorious. Also fabulous at sunset are the **Arizona Steakhouse**, next door at Thunderbird Lodge, and the **Grand Canyon Lodge** dining room on the North Rim. Menus feature some unusual starters and a nightly cream soup, followed by entrees that include filet mignon, chicken, lamb, local trout, and wild salmon prepared continental-style. There's always at least one vegetarian dish, usually pasta. Desserts tend to be lavish and rich. The wine list includes some bottles from southern Arizona's wine country.

You'll pay a lot, but don't expect miracles. The kitchens in all park restaurants feed large numbers daily, so quality can be variable. Stick with meat or vegetarian, and avoid fish that can get overcooked and dry between the kitchen and table.

Tusayan Eateries

The wait for a table at El Tovar and Arizona Steakhouse can be prohibitive without an advance reservation. If that's the case, your best bet is to drive to nearby **Tusayan.** The **Coronado Room** restaurant inside the Best Western Grand Canyon Squire Inn on the south end of town is a surprisingly pleasant and relaxed place for a meal, with high-quality continental dining and attentive service.

If you're looking for entertainment, the twice-nightly dinner show at the **Canyon Star** restaurant in the Grand Hotel opposite is pretty much the only option. The menu here has a few winners, including a nicely presented elk tenderloin and pasta primavera, but so-so service and the overly casual atmosphere rule this out as a place for a special meal. While you eat, a Navajo Indian family performs dances on the large dance floor and a host explains a bit about the culture. Some of the bar stools here have saddles instead of seats.

The predominantly Mexican waitstaff seem more engaged at the self-service buffet in the lobby of the **Quality Inn**, which offers speedy supplementary service at breakfast and an evening selection of entrees that brings in locals as well as tourists. **Jennifer's Internet Bakery Cafe** has the best light breakfasts, home-made pastries, sandwiches, and coffee drinks in town, but closes at 5pm. Special trail mix selections and iced herbal tea drinks can be purchased at **Happy Trails**, across the street. For a small fee you can surf the internet at Jennifer's and Happy Trails while dining.

On the Road

The large selection of restaurants in **Flagstaff** owes much to the town's location at the junction of Interstates 40 and 17 and Highways 89 and 180 to Grand Canyon, as well as the presence of Northern Arizona University. The quaint downtown, north and south of the tracks, has a number of old favorites. **Pasto** features excellent Italian food, **Cafe Espress** is known for its vegetarian specials, and there's a surprisingly good Thai restaurant in the historic **Monte Vista Hotel**. The **Late for the Train** and **Macy's** coffee houses, which roast their own beans, are always busy at breakfast time. Next door to Macy's, on Beaver Street, is **Bellavia**, one of Flag's most popular breakfast spots.

Coffee at Macy's

The food gets decidedly fancy in **Sedona**, where the high-end resorts attract a sophisticated crowd. The family-owned **Heartline Cafe**, in the center, is Sedona's best-loved restaurant. It has won quite a loyal following for its continental-style cuisine and laid-back garden atmosphere.

One of the main highlights of **Route 66** are the diners along the route. These are not only good places to eat but also to meet the people who live on Route 66. Establishments such as **Mr. D'z Route 66 Diner** in Kingman are well known for their retro ambiance.

HANDY TRAVEL TIPS

An A–Z Summary of Practical Information

US Forest Service and Bureau of Land Management campgrounds are usually 'primitive', meaning they have designated sites and picnic tables, but usually only vault toilets. Many campgrounds have no water, so keep a 5–gallon (22-liter) water carrier in the car.

Dispersed camping is allowed for free on national forest lands, but you need a permit from the Backcountry Information Center to camp at the bottom of the canyon *(see page 120)*. Bring all you'll need. Aside from food and water, the most useful items are moist babywipes for general hygiene, plastic bags for trash, toilet paper, and a small trowel for digging a 6-in (15-cm) cat hole to bury human waste.

Campgrounds. Mather Campground at the South Rim is $18 per site per night. Desert View Campground is $10 per night. RV campgrounds with hookups include Trailer Village (from $25 per night) and Ten-X Campground, 2 miles (3km) south of Tusayan ($10 per night, no hookups or showers. The North Rim Campground is open May to mid-October and costs $18–25 per night. De Motte and Jacob Lake Campgrounds, operated by the US Forest Service, are off Highway 67. Kaibab Camper Village is half a mile (1km) south of Jacob Lake. Reservations are advisable for park campgrounds and may be made up to five months in advance (tel: 800-365-2267; outside the US, tel: 301-722-1257, <www.nps.gov/grca>).

CAR RENTAL/HIRE (see also DRIVING on page 116)

Car rental companies are located at Phoenix Airport and in tourist towns like Sedona, Flagstaff, and Tusayan. Rates for a subcompact generally start at $25 per day; SUVs such as Ford Explorers, Chevy Broncos, and Lincoln Navigators are about $100 per day. Most companies offer unlimited mileage. For information on renting an RV, contact Recreational Vehicle Rental Association (tel: 800-336-035 <www.rvra.org>).

You will need a valid US or international driver's license and a major credit card to rent a car and the minimum age is 21. Some companies will not rent to drivers under 25. If you're visiting from overseas, plan on buying accident insurance. Most US drivers will find they are covered under their personal plan, but check first: in the event of an accident, you will be required to pay upfront for repairs. Expect to pay an additional $15–25 per day.

CLIMATE (See also HIKING on page 120)

Northern Arizona has about 266 days of sunshine annually. Yearly rainfall averages 12½in (30cm); nearly all of it falls as snow in winter and brief, intense thunderstorms in the summer, when dry sandy washes, *arroyos* (gullies) and narrow rock-walled canyons are prone to flash floods. Wind velocity in cities is under 8mph (13kph) but exposed and high-elevation areas can be very gusty. In summer, the South Rim of the Grand Canyon can reach 90°F (32°C), with temperatures about 20°F (11°C) warmer at the bottom of the gorge. During 'monsoon' season, between July and September, avoid hiking or camping in *arroyos* and don't try to cross a flash-flooding river or stream on foot or in a car.

The weather is more comfortable in spring and fall, with average daytime highs between 65°F (18°C) and 75°F (24°C). Springtime winds can be very strong, though, as the jetstream changes direction from the northwest to the south, via the Gulf of California, the source of all those tropical storms in summer. Nights are chilly.

Winter temperatures are often below freezing and can dip significantly at night. Snowstorms are frequent, but the inner gorge can remain relatively warm and mild. Expect icy conditions on roads and trails and occasional road closings due to snow.

The North Rim is about 1,000ft (300m) higher than the South Rim and is much cooler and breezier, with summer highs around 75°F (24°C). Evening and morning can be nippy. The North Rim is blanketed with as much as 200in (510cm) of snow in winter and is closed from mid-October to mid-May.

CLOTHING (See also HIKING on page 120)

With few exceptions, people dress informally here. A pair of jeans or slacks, a button-down polo or T-shirt, and boots or shoes are appropriate for all but the fanciest places and events. Shorts and light shirts are suitable for most situations in the warmer months (although you should dress more modestly if you attend Indian dances). You'll need a sweater for evenings, high elevations, and overly air-conditioned shops and restaurants. Synthetic fleece sweaters are a good idea: they're light, don't wrinkle, and stay warm when wet. Bring a lightweight, breathable rain jacket to keep you dry during summer 'monsoon' downpours.

A pair of sturdy hiking shoes or boots that you've already worn in are essential. Thin, inner polypropylene socks and thick, outer socks will help keep your feet dry and comfortable. If blisters or sore spots develop, quickly cover them with moleskin or surgical tape, available at most pharmacies or camping supply stores. River shoes or sport sandals with strong Velcro ties and arch support are a useful addition to your traveling wardrobe. Even if you don't plan on doing a river or lake trip, many hiking trails require you to cross streams and get your feet wet. Flip-flops just won't cut it.

Don't underestimate the power of the sun in the high desert, even on cloudy days. Sunscreen with a minimum sunblock factor of 15 is essential year round, as are a wide-brimmed hat, long-sleeved cotton shirt and pants for covering up, polarized sunglasses, and a cotton bandanna that can be soaked to keep major arteries cool (be sure to cover your neck with a bandanna if you wear a baseball cap). Some companies now make clothing with a built-in mesh sunscreen.

CUSTOMS AND ENTRY REQUIREMENTS

Canadians entering from the western hemisphere, Mexicans with border passes, and British residents of Bermuda and Canada do not normally need a visa or passport. Citizens of the UK, Australia, New Zealand, and the Republic of Ireland no longer need a visa for

stays of less than 90 days, but only a valid passport and a return airline ticket. The airline will issue a visa waiver form. Citizens of
South Africa need a visa – check with your local US consulate or
embassy and allow three weeks for delivery.

Duty-free allowance. You will be asked to complete a customs dec-
laration form before you arrive in the US. Restrictions are as follows: you are generally allowed to bring in a reasonable amount of
tobacco and alcohol for your personal use. A non-resident may
claim, free of duty and taxes, articles up to $400 (£200) in value for
use as gifts for other persons. The exemption is only valid if the
gifts accompany you, you stay 72 hours or more, and have not
claimed this exemption within the preceding six months. Up to 100
cigars may be included within this gift exemption. (Cuban cigars,
however, are forbidden and may be confiscated.) Arriving and de-
parting passengers must report any money or checks, etc. exceed-
ing a total of $10,000 (£5,000). Agricultural products, meat, and
animals are subject to complex restrictions, particularly if you are
entering from California.

Note: Tightened security measures cause delays at most airports.
Allow at least two hours for domestic flights, three hours for international flights. Penknives, nail clippers, and cigarette lighters are
not permitted in carry-on luggage. To speed through security, place
all items in see-through bags in suitcases and be prepared to open
laptop computers and other carry-on luggage.

D

DRIVING (See also CAR RENTAL/HIRE on page 113)

Scenic driving is a major activity in northern Arizona *(see page 85)*.
In the US, driving is on the right. The speed limit in cities and national parks is 30mph (50kph) unless otherwise indicated, usually
55–65mph (90–108kph) on state highways, unless otherwise indi-

able at Grand Canyon Village and Hermit's Rest; toilet at Hopi Point. Access via shuttles.

• **South Kaibab Trail to Cedar Ridge.** Difficult, steep, and very exposed but best for a quick inner-canyon hike in summer; 3 miles (5km) round trip; 1,140ft (350m) elevation change. Highlights include spectacular views of Tonto Platform and Inner Gorge. Overnight hikes to Phantom Ranch (7 miles/11km one way) require backcountry permits. No water on trail. Toilet at Cedar Ridge. Heavy use by mules and through-canyon hikers.

• **Bright Angel Trail to Indian Gardens.** Steep, difficult, but better shaded than other trails; 9.2-mile (14.8-km) round-trip hike and 3,000ft (915m) elevation change to Indian Gardens. 1½ Mile Rest House and 3 Mile Rest House have toilets and water from May to September (check for pipe breaks). The 9.6-mile (15.5-km) one-way hike to river requires overnight permit. Heavy use by mules and through-canyon hikers.

• **Hermit Trail to Hermit/Dripping Springs Junction.** Very steep, difficult, and exposed part of trail; 3½ miles (5.6km) round trip, climbs 1,440ft (440m). No water or toilets. Highlights include springs in pretty side canyon that was home to the hermit miner Louis Boucher.

• **Grandview Point to Coconino Saddle.** Very steep, difficult, exposed, and unmaintained trail built by miner John Hance; 1½ miles (2.5km) round trip and 1,165ft (355m) elevation change. Highlights include shallower East Rim vistas and sunrise views of Painted Desert. For seasoned desert hikers only (not recommended as a day hike in summer). No water. Toilet at Horseshoe Mesa. Trail begins 12 miles (19km) east of Grand Canyon Village on Desert View Drive.

North Rim

• **Transept Trail, Grand Canyon Lodge to North Rim Campground.** An easy 3-mile (5-km) round-trip hike with no elevation change. Dense forest, side canyon views. No water or toilets on trail.

• **North Kaibab Trail to Supai Tunnel.** Steep, difficult, but adequately shaded 5.4-mile (8.7-km) round-trip hike; 1,415ft (430m) elevation change. Moderate grades and lack of crowds make this the best inner canyon hike for beginners. Highlights include forest vistas and views of Bright Angel and Roaring Springs Canyons. Water and toilets at Supai Tunnel (2.7 miles/4.4km). The 14 miles (22.5km) to the river cannot be hiked in a day; overnight permit required.

• **Uncle Jim Trail.** Easy, forested rim trail; 5-mile (8-km) round-trip, no elevation loss. Named for first Grand Canyon game warden. Highlights are cool forest vistas and canyon overlook. No water or toilets on trail. Starts at North Kaibab trailhead. Used by mules.

Sedona/Oak Creek Red Rock Country

• **West Fork of Oak Creek (Call of the Canyon) Trail.** Easy to moderate 3-mile (5-km) round-trip summer hike in scenic red rock river canyon; no elevation change. Water, toilets, fee at trailhead.

Arizona-Utah Border

• **Paria River Canyon Trail, Lees Ferry to Paria, Utah.** Difficult summer hike through deep river-carved sandstone canyon with wading and backcountry camping; 38 miles (61km) one way, so allow 4–6 days. For experienced desert canyon hikers. Permit required.

HOLIDAYS

The following are national holidays in the US. Banks, offices, and some stores are closed on these days. *Note:* National parks are usually only closed on Christmas Day and New Year's Day.

New Year's Day	1 January
Martin Luther King Day	Third Monday in January
President's Day	Third Monday in February
Memorial Day	Last Monday in May
Independence Day	4 July
Labor Day	First Monday in September
Columbus Day	Second Monday in October

Veterans' Day	11 November
Thanksgiving Day	Fourth Thursday in November
Christmas Day	25 December

L

LAUNDRY AND DRY CLEANING

Coin-op laundries are located next to the Mather Campground on the South Rim, and the North Rim Campground; hours 7am–9pm. Dry cleaning outlets are in Grand Canyon Village and Flagstaff.

LOST PROPERTY

For items lost in hotels or restaurants in Grand Canyon National Park, tel: 928-638-2631. For all other lost items, tel: 928- 638-7798. Take found items to the Visitor Center at Canyon View Information Plaza.

M

MEDIA

Radio and Television. Almost all northern Arizona hotel rooms have cable or satellite television, including CNN, ABC, NBC, CBS and PBS. Public radio KNAU broadcasts from Northern Arizona University, and includes all-day classical music, *All Things Considered*, *Fresh Air*, and other favorites. KAFF broadcasts country music.

Magazines and Newspapers. The *Guide,* two separate park newspapers for the South and North Rim, is published twice-yearly by **Grand Canyon Association** (tel: 928-638-7027, <www.grand canyon.org>), the park's non-profit partner and publisher of a variety of educational books on the Grand Canyon. The *Guide* has complete information on park facilities and programs, maps, and articles and is free with admission. A Grand Canyon *Trip Planner* and other information for planning your visit are available by contacting the **National Park Service** (P.O. Box 129, Grand Canyon, AZ 86023, tel: 928-638-7888, <www.nps.gov/grca>).

The *Arizona Daily Sun* is the daily newspaper for the Northland; the *Arizona Republic* covers the whole state. *Arizona Highways* magazine, a state-run tourism magazine, has many beautiful photo essays and interesting articles on Arizona.

MONEY

Currency. The dollar is divided into 100 cents. The coins are as follows: 1 cent (penny), 5 cents (nickel), 10 cents (dime), 25 cents (quarter), and $1 (new in 2000). Bank notes (bills) of $1, $5, $10, $20, $50, $100 are common, but some establishments will not accept denominations over $20 unless you make a large purchase.

Credit cards. The major cards are widely accepted at Grand Canyon and elsewhere but not usually by individual vendors on the Indian reservations. Carry some cash with you for paying for goods and services and tipping on the reservations.

Exchange facilities. Banks in the area are usually open weekdays from 9am–3pm. Some open on Saturdays. Bank One is a full-service bank in Grand Canyon Village *(see Banks and* ATMs *on page 110)*. You can exchange travelers' checks here.

ATMs. These are widely available. However, most banks charge non-account holders a fee, and your own bank will also levy a fee for use of another bank's ATM. Try to use your own bank.

Sales Tax. There is no VAT in the US. A sales tax is added to purchases, currently between 6 and 7 percent of sale.

Travelers' Checks. Travelers' checks denominated in US dollars are best. Foreign currency travelers' checks must be exchanged at a bank.

O

OPENING HOURS

Information centers at the South Rim of the Grand Canyon are open during the following hours:

Canyon View Information Plaza Visitor Center: 8am–5pm.

Yavapai Observation Station: 8am–7pm in summer, until 5pm in winter.

Kolb Studio: 8am–6pm.

Tusayan Museum: 9am–4pm.

Desert View Bookstore/Park Information: 9am–5pm, as staffing permits.

P

PHOTOGRAPHY AND DVD

All popular brands of film and photographic equipment are available. Pre-recorded DVDs bought in the US will not work in Europe unless you have a multi-region DVD player.

POLICE

In an emergency, call 911 or contact the nearest park ranger.

POST OFFICES

Grand Canyon Post Office (tel: 928-638-2512) is located in Market Plaza in Grand Canyon Village. Window service: Mon–Thurs 9am–4.30pm and Sat 11am–3pm. Lobby service: 5am–10pm for purchase of stamps. A post office is also located adjacent to Grand Canyon Lodge on the North Rim.

PRECAUTIONS

Insurance. It's vital to have health insurance in the US. Foreign visitors should buy travelers' insurance before leaving.

Flash floods. Don't hike or camp in dry washes or narrow canyons in summer, when daily thunderstorms cause frequent flash floods. If a road is flooded, wait for the water to subside. Never try to drive through it.

Sunburn. Wear a high SPF-factor sunscreen to avoid burning at this high elevation.

Drinking water. Purify all water from natural sources before drinking, due to the presence of **giardia** bacteria. Either use a filter or purification tablets, or boil water for at least 15 minutes.

Dehydration. It's essential to drink enough water in the desert, especially when active outdoors. In summer, carry and drink a gallon (4.5 liters) of water per person per day on day hikes, and at least two pints (1 liter) on short hikes. Cut down on caffeine and alcohol to avoid dehydration.

Hyponatremia. When hiking, make sure you eat enough salty, high-energy food along with your water to avoid diluting minerals essential to metabolism.

Altitude sickness. This can be a significant problem on the Colorado Plateau, where elevations are between 5,000ft and 12,000ft (1,500m and 3,600m). Acclimatize slowly, if possible, and don't overexert yourself, even if you're young and fit.

Heat exhaustion and heatstroke. These occur when the body overheats in hot, dry conditions; both are exacerbated by long hours of strenuous hiking or other exercise – a common problem for hikers in the Grand Canyon. If you begin to feel dizzy, weak, and have clammy pale skin, stop, rest, drink lots of water and have a snack, before continuing slowly.

A red, dry face coupled with the above are symptoms of life-threatening heatstroke, when the body core overheats dangerously and cannot cool down. It's a common problem with light-skinned people from northern latitudes. Immediately immerse yourself in cool (not cold) water. Wear wet clothing and carry a spray bottle to avoid problems.

T

TELEPHONE/FAX

Telephones. You can dial directory assistance (tel: 411 or 1 + the area code + 555 + 1212) or an operator (dial 0) for free from any payphone. All numbers with 800, 888, 877 prefix are toll-free. For domestic long-distance calls in the US, dial 1 + the area code + the 7-digit number. For international calls, dial 011 + the country code + the number.

The area code in northern Arizona is 928. Local calls cost 25 cents for the first three minutes, after which, if you are in a payphone, the operator will tell you to add more money. Most newsstands and drug stores sell phone or calling cards for long-distance calls. A good way to avoid the hefty surcharges that hotels add to outgoing calls is to use a calling card with a payphone.

Fax. You can send a fax from many of the hotels in the area, but it is very expensive. It is cheaper to send a fax from a Mailboxes Etc, or FedExKinko's, both of which have outlets in Flagstaff.

Telegraph. A telegraph is available at Canyon Food Mart in Tusayan.

Internet. Several places in Tusayan have internet access, including Grand Canyon Tourist Center, Happy Trails, Quality Inn, Red Feather Lodge, and Jennifer's Internet Bakery Cafe. Many hotels provide an internet service, ask at the reception desk.

TIME ZONES

Arizona is on Mountain Standard Time. The state and the Hopi reservation do not observe Daylight Savings Time (between April and October), when clocks 'spring' forward; the time is the same as Pacific Standard Time during that period.

Note: The Navajo Nation and Lake Powell National Recreation Area, which include areas in the neighboring states of New Mexico and Utah, do observe Daylight Savings Time.

TIPPING

Service is never included in restaurant prices, but it is sometimes added to your bill for parties of six or more. Tip 15–20 percent in restaurants; about the same for taxi drivers, spa and beauty services. Porters should be tipped $1 per bag. Don't forget tour guides (10–15 percent) and chamber maids (a few dollars a day). Low-paid service jobs in the tourism industry are the norm on the Colorado Plateau and workers rely on tips to make up the shortfall.

TOURIST INFORMATION

Canyon View Information Center is the main visitor center at the South Rim of Grand Canyon National Park. Rangers help visitors plan their trips and offer daily programs. Outdoor exhibits, open 24 hours, include information on hiking, tours, and other activities. Other park information centers include **Yavapai Observation Station, Desert View, Tusayan Museum,** and the seasonal **North Rim Visitor Center**.

For regional information on national parks, contact the National Park Service offices in Phoenix (tel: 602-640-5250). You can also get information on the park in Tusayan through the Arizona Tourism help desk in the **Grand Canyon IMAX Theater** and **Grand Canyon Chamber of Commerce** (tel: 928-638-2901).

Other tourism offices include Flagstaff Convention and Visitor Bureau (tel: 928-779-7611), Page-Lake Powell Visitor Bureau (tel: 888-261-7243), Sedona Chamber of Commerce (tel: 800-288-7336), and Williams-Grand Canyon Chamber of Commerce (tel: 928-635-4061). Arizona Office of Tourism (tel: 888-520-3433) in Phoenix can help with statewide queries. Call Navajo Nation Tourism Office (tel: 928-871-6436) in Window Rock for information on the Navajo reservation.

TRAVELERS WITH DISABILITIES

Paved trails suitable for use by travelers with disabilities can be found in many parks, including the Grand Canyon. Wheelchairs are

Today it offers 20 guest rooms furnished in spare but elegant style of the period and named after such famous guests as Bob Hope, Carol Lombard, and Howard Hughes. The rambling public spaces are filled with historic photographs, bric-a-brac, and the owners' artwork. The restaurant serves elegant southwest food. Rooms on the north side avoid track noise.

Radisson Woodlands Hotel Flagstaff $$–$$$ *1175 West Route 66, Flagstaff, AZ 86001; tel: 928-773-8888 or toll free 800-333-3333; <www.radisson.com>.* Flagstaff's most elegant hotel, the Woodlands is a modern property located on the west side of town, near shops, movie theaters, and restaurants. The lobby has Italian marble floors, granite architectural details, and plush European-style furnishings. Guest rooms are spacious and tasteful. You can eat some of the best sushi in town at its Japanese restaurant and sushi bar. Two restaurants, outdoor pool, fitness center.

SEDONA AND ENVIRONS

Amara Creekside Resort $$$–$$$$ *310 N. Highway 89A, Sedona, AZ; tel: 866-455-6610; <www.amararesort.com>.* Amara has a young, hip, casual ambiance that will appeal to Europeans and world travelers. The 99 rooms have a Zen calm with cream walls, elegant beds, coffee-makers and fridges, and marble bathrooms. Rooms either overlook the creek or have patios or balconies opening onto the lawn. Amenities include restaurant, pool, whirlpool, and fitness room. WiFi throughout.

Briar Patch Inn $$$$ *3190 N. Highway 89A, Sedona, AZ 86336; tel: 928-282-2342 or toll free 888-809-3030; <www.briarpatch inn.com>.* This delightful cabin resort on the shady banks of Oak Creek, just north of Sedona, occupies an old homestead and has beautifully maintained historic cabins with Western decor. When the sun goes down in this deep canyon, the in-room fireplaces are a particularly nice touch. Organic breakfasts are served on the patio in summer; on weekends, local musicians play classical music (in-room CD players offer a selection of their CDs). Massages are available in the outdoor gazebo next to the creek. Expensive but worth it.

INDIAN RESERVATIONS

Cameron Trading Post Motel $$ *Highway 89, P.O. Box 339, Cameron, AZ 86020; tel: 928-679-2231 or toll free 800-338-7385; <www.camerontradingpost.com>.* This 100-room motel adjoins a busy historic trading post at the bridge over the Little Colorado River on the Navajo Nation. Rooms are comfortable, and the restaurant excellent. Restaurant, gift shop, post office, gas station.

Gouldings Lodge $$–$$$ *P.O. Box 360001, Monument Valley, UT 84536; tel: 435-727-3231; <www.gouldings.com>.* Harry and Mike Goulding's historic trading post offers the only motel accommodations in Monument Valley. The hotel can arrange horseback and Jeep tours with Navajo guides. The onsite restaurant has standard food but great views. Amenities include restaurant, gift shop, indoor pool, tour desk, museum, supermarket, ATM, gas station, in-room VCRs and videos of movies shot in Monument Valley.

Hualapai Lodge $$ *900 Route 66, P.O. Box 538, Peach Springs, AZ 86434; tel: 888-255-9550 or toll free 888-255-9550; <www.hualapai tours.com>.* An expected bit of luxury in a spare region, this 60-room hotel has attractive rooms, a large pleasant lobby and fireplace, and a good dining room. Tours of Grand Canyon West leave from here. Amenities include restaurant, tour desk, laundry.

Supai Lodge $$ *P.O. Box 159, Supai, AZ 86435; tel: 928-448-2111 or 928-448 2201; <www.havasupaitribe.com>.* The only lodging inside the western end of Grand Canyon, this motel on the Havasupai reservation is only accessible on foot or horseback. It has no phones or TVs. All 24 rooms are non-smoking and have two double beds; roll-away beds are available.

Thunderbird Lodge $$ *P.O. Box 548, Chinle, AZ 86503; tel: 928-674-5841 or toll free 800-679-2473; <www.tbirdlodge.com>.* Well-maintained, family-run accommodation on shady grounds near the visitor center at Canyon de Chelly ('de-shay') National Monument. Amenities include cafeteria, gift shop, Jeep tours, and Navajo guides to show you around the park.

Recommended Restaurants

With a few exceptions, Grand Canyon restaurants are geared toward middle American tastes, and food is often bland, overcooked, and plentiful. Make dinner reservations when you book a room to avoid long waits. Flagstaff and Sedona are great places to eat out. Both towns have lots of bakery cafes, ethnic establishments serving everything from authentic Mexican, East Indian, and Thai food to Italian, and even a few upscale restaurants known for their innovative cuisine.

The price categories are based on the average cost of a three-course meal for one, not including drinks, tax, or tip. Many restaurants include soup or salad with the price of entree. All restaurants take major credit cards unless noted.

$$$	$40 and up
$$	$20–40
$	under $20

SOUTH RIM

Arizona Room $–$$ *Bright Angel Lodge, Grand Canyon, AZ 86023; tel: 928-638-2631.* A good second choice if El Tovar is full, this middle-of-the-road steakhouse has equally wonderful sunset views of the canyon. The menu features steak, grilled chicken, and fish. Arrive early for lunch or dinner as reservations aren't taken here. Open 11.30am–10pm.

Bright Angel Restaurant $ *Bright Angel Lodge, Grand Canyon, AZ 86023; tel: 928-638-2631.* Diner food – indifferently prepared and served – is offered at this coffee shop. Ideal fare for fussy children as the menu concentrates on familiar choices like breakfast eggs, burgers, steaks, patty melts, spaghetti, and chili. The burger and fries may be your best bet. You can work it off on the trail. Open 6.30am–10pm.

Delicatessen at Marketplace $ *Market Plaza, Grand Canyon, AZ 86023.* Since being taken over by concessionaire Delaware North, this deli in the South Rim's main grocery store has begun to serve some very decent food, and now may be your best bet for a quick bite. You'll find tasty meat chili served in a sourdough bread bowl, fresh-roasted chicken and turkey sandwiches, salads, fruit, yogurt, and other filling but healthy choices. The coffee here is Seattle's Best. Open 8am–7pm.

El Tovar Dining Room $$–$$$ *El Tovar Hotel, Grand Canyon, AZ 86023; tel: 928-638-2631 ext. 6432.* As good as it gets on the South Rim, which is to say not fantastic but not bad. The rustic dining room is fetching, with dark-paneled walls and Indian murals, crisp white linen and silver on tables, and attentive waitstaff. But the food, which leans toward rich Continental dishes laced with southwest accents, is uneven. Despite huge efforts to achieve gourmet dining on the Rim, it's impossible to guarantee consistency in such a busy restaurant. Ask for a table near the huge picture window at sunset. Make dinner reservations weeks in advance or plan on eating very late, when most Americans are in bed. Open 6.30am–10 pm.

NORTH RIM AND ENVIRONS

Grand Canyon Lodge Dining Room $$ *Grand Canyon Lodge, Bright Angel Point, North Rim, Grand Canyon, AZ; tel: (928) 638-2611.* The only fully-fledged restaurant on the North Rim is set in a grand, window-wrapped room on the edge of the canyon. The menu is dominated by American and Continental dishes, such as prime rib, rosemary chicken, pasta in pesto sauce with asparagus, and the like. The food is not particularly memorable, and the service (as elsewhere at the park, where low-paid seasonal staff are the norm) is inconsistent. But that view! Be sure to dine early enough to enjoy it. Make dinner reservations weeks ahead. Closed Nov–May.

Jacob Lake Inn $ *Highway 67 and 89A, Jacob Lake, AZ 86022; tel: 928-643-7232.* The inn's chummy coffee shop is a welcome break during a long, lonesome traverse of the Arizona Strip. There's a dining room with regular table service but the old-fashioned counter is more fun. The menu features Mormon family recipes such as southwest baked chicken, jagerschnitzel, and baked local trout. You can never go wrong with the burger and fries. The baked goods (especially home-made pies) are scrumptious, and the milk-shakes (ask for extra thick) are a meal in themselves.

Lees Ferry Lodge $–$$ *Highway 89A, Marble Canyon, AZ; tel: 928-355-2231.* Simple, hearty American fare served in a rustic wood-paneled dining room makes this small Western lodge a popu-lar haunt for river rafters and guides who are preparing to launch onto 'the Grand'. An extensive selection of beers is available, and the wine list is an unexpected pleasure.

Rainbow Room $$ *Wahweap Lodge, 100 Lakeshore Drive, Page, AZ; tel: 928-645-1162.* This large resort complex just west of Glen Canyon Dam is a busy place. The restaurant has wonderful views of adjoining Lake Powell, a hotspot with Arizonans on weekends. Cuisine is mainly American and Continental. Bullfrog Marina, on the Utah side of the lake, has a similar lodge complex with a pleas-ant view from the dining room.

Fernando's Hideaway $ *332 N. 300 West Street, Kanab, UT; tel: 435-644-3222.* Slightly off the main drag in Kanab, this neighbor-hood Mexican restaurant serves unexpectedly good food. Dine on the patio or inside, where there's a fresh southwestern ambiance, with tile floors, and whitewashed walls adorned with Mexican folk art. The consistently good food, killer Margaritas, and inexpensive prices make this a restaurant that locals recommend to visitors time and again.

Rocking V Cafe $–$$$ *97 W. Center Street, Kanab, UT; tel: 435-644-8001.* Kanab's most sophisticated restaurant serves up some unexpected gems including wild Alaskan salmon, flown in four times a week in season. The menu also has filet mignon, rib-eye steaks, and lots of vegetarian and vegan items. The dessert specialty is creme brulée. At lunch, choose from soups, salads, and burgers. Closed Jan and Feb. Open Mon and Tues in March, Nov, and Dec.

TUSAYAN

Canyon Star Restaurant $$ *The Grand Hotel, Grand Canyon, AZ 86023; tel: 928-638-3333.* The cavernous cowboy-themed dining room in this park lodge-style hotel offers twice-nightly dinner shows with Indian dancing on a center stage. Waitstaff are indifferent but a few dishes show surprising flair considering they're not the main focus. The seared elk tenderloin with berry reduction puts you in the mood for Native entertainment.

Coronado Room $$–$$$ *Best Western Grand Canyon Squire Inn, Grand Canyon, AZ 86023; tel: 928-638-2681.* An excellent alternative in nearby Tusayan if all the South Rim restaurants have long lines. American and Continental fare is done well, and includes filet mignon, salmon, spare ribs, and such novelties as frogs' legs. Excellent service and a friendly ambiance.

Jennifer's Internet Bakery Cafe $ *Highway 64, Grand Canyon.* This tiny bakery has good coffee drinks, home-made pastries, some nice breakfast egg dishes, bagel and sandwiches, and the closest approximation to a hip atmosphere in bland Tusayan. Closes at 5pm. The Mexican staff can help you log onto the internet for a small fee.

FLAGSTAFF AND ENVIRONS

Beaver Street Brewery $ *11 S. Beaver Street, Flagstaff; tel: 928-779-0079.* One of several brewpubs in Flagstaff, Beaver Street has an assortment of frothy home-brew, from a robust stout to a light berry ale. The delicious wood-fired pizza, gooey fondue, and bar food are popular with the university crowd down the street.

Black Bean Burrito and Salsa Company $ *12 E. Route 66, Flagstaff; tel: 928-779-9905.* A tasty variety of rib-sticking burritos are the specialty here, served in foil and plastic and eaten at the counter. ¡Muy sabroso! (Very tasty!)

Cafe Espress $ *16 N. San Francisco Street, Flagstaff; tel: 928-774-0541.* A long-established favorite with the outdoors crowd, this arty, laid-back cafe offers fresh, healthy, somewhat eccentric food ranging from *huevos rancheros* and other filling Mexican specialties to vegetarian dishes such as spanakopita, mushroom stroganoff, and artichoke scampi. The baked goods and desserts are yummy.

Charly's Pub & Grill $ *23 N. Leroux Street, Flagstaff; tel: 928-774-8431.* Located on the ground floor of the historic Weatherford Hotel, off Heritage Square, which once hosted writer Zane Grey, Charly's Pub & Grill is a great spot to indulge in some people-watching on a warm summer's evening. The bistro-style menu features a number of reasonably priced and reliable southwestern dishes, such as burritos, *posole*, Navajo tacos, and homemade soups, salads, bread, and pies. Good selection of wines.

Cottage Place Restaurant $$–$$$ *126 W. Cottage Avenue, Flagstaff; tel: 928-774-8431.* This intimate little restaurant housed in a renovated 1909 bungalow is a bit on the showy side – white tablecloths, starchy waiters, and service with a flourish. American-Continental dishes include charbroiled tiger shrimp, lobster tail and Chateaubriand. Vegetarians catered for. Reservations required. Dinner only Tues–Sun.

Cowboy Club $$ *241 Highway 89A, Sedona; tel: 928-282-4200.* Cowboy cuisine with an upmarket Sedona twist. Ribs, meatloaf, and juicy steaks go all 'nouvelle western' here and join fried nopal cactus pads, rattlesnake, and buffalo on an eclectic menu that appeals to visitors. A Sedona institution.

Heartline Cafe $$ *1610 Highway 89A, Sedona; tel: 928-282-0785.* Chuck and Phyllis Cline opened this pretty restaurant in 1991 and have been so successful that they've even written their own cookbook. Heartline has an inventive menu, which leans heavily toward Continental dishes with southwest touches. Favorites are the rich pecan-crusted trout with Dijon cream, chicken breast with prickly pear sauce, and tequila-lime marinated salmon with pesto quesadilla. Accompany entrees with a nice wine from southern Arizona, and you'll have the perfect southwest dining experience. Reservations recommended.

Macy's European Coffee House and Bakery $ *14 S. Beaver Street, Flagstaff; tel: 928-774-2243.* Both faculty staff and students at the nearby university hang out at this classic college-town coffee house run by Tim Macy, who roasts his own beans to dark French Roast perfection. An array of muffins, bear claws, strudels, and other pastries are freshly baked each morning. More substantial breakfast, lunch, and dinner dishes are available.

Pasto $–$$ *19 E. Aspen Street, Flagstaff; tel: 928-779-1937.* The previous owners of Cafe Espress are onto a winner with this hip Italian restaurant around the corner. A good place for a pleasurable dinner with friends that won't break the bank. Look for unusual dishes such as black-bean ravioli with your choice of sauces, including a killer garlicky pesto.

INDIAN RESERVATIONS

Hopi Cultural Center Restaurant $ *Second Mesa; tel: 928-734-2401.* You'll meet Hopi residents dining on standard American fare at this reservation restaurant next to the museum. Visitors will be more interested in the Pueblo specialties, such as paper-thin piki bread and blue-corn pancakes and mutton stew.

Molly Butler Lodge $–$$ *109 Main Street, Greer; tel: 928-735-7226.* Mormon pioneers Molly and John Butler built their early 1900s' homestead in Greer, a tiny forested community in the White Mountains next to the Apache reservation. While John served as hunting guide to Theodore Roosevelt and writer Zane Grey, Molly was famous for her home cooking. The food here is still worth an overnight trip to one of Greer's cabin resorts. Try the aged steaks, prime rib, and perfectly cooked halibut. All are accompanied by baked potato, salad, fresh veggies, and a hot mini-loaf of delicious white bread.

Thunderbird Lodge $ *Chinle, AZ 86503; tel: 928-674-5841.* Set at the edge of Canyon de Chelly, the original stone trading post now serves as a cafeteria. The food is cheap and simple, and the walls are hung with beautiful Navajo rugs that are all for sale.

INDEX